VIOLENCE

*A gift
from the library of
Pastor Carol A. Nolte*

VIOLENCE

The Unrelenting Assault on Human Dignity

Wolfgang Huber

Translated by Ruth C. L. Gritsch

Foreword by Daniel Berrigan, S.J.

FORTRESS PRESS

Minneapolis

VIOLENCE
The Unrelenting Assault on Human Dignity

First Fortress Press edition 1996. Translated by Ruth C. L. Gritsch from the German *Die tägliche Gewalt: Gegen den Ausverkauf der Menschenwürde* (Freiburg im Breisgau, Verlag Herder, © 1993). Translation copyright © 1996 Augsburg Fortress Publishers.

Scripture quotations unless otherwise noted are from the Revised Standard Version of the Bible, copyright © 1946, 1971, and 1973 by the Division of Christian Education of the National Council of Churches of Christ in the U.S.A. Used by permission.

Cover design: Brad Norr Design
Text design: David Lott

Library of Congress Cataloging-in-Publication Data

Huber, Wolfgang, 1942–
    [Tägliche Gewalt. English]
    Violence : the unrelenting assault on human dignity / Wolfgang
    Huber ; translated by Ruth C. L. Gritsch ; foreword by Daniel
    Berrigan.
        p. cm.
    Includes bibliographical references and index.
    ISBN 0-8006-2858-6 (alk. paper)
    1. Violence—Religious aspects—Christianity. 2. Man (Christian
    theology) I. Title.
    BT736.15.H8313 1996
    241'.697—dc20
                                                              96–26623
                                                                   CIP

The paper used in this publication meets the minimum requirements of American National Standard for Information Sciences—Permanence of Paper for Printed Library Materials, ANSI Z329.48-1984.

Manufactured in the U.S.A.   AF–2858

00   99   98   97   96   1   2   3   4   5   6   7   8   9   10

For Kara
after three decades
with grateful love

Contents

Foreword   *Daniel Berrigan, S.J.*   xi

Preface to the American Edition   *Wolfgang Huber*   xv

Introduction: Our Daily Violence   1
    Forms of Violence
    Responsible Lifestyles
    The Process of Clarification

Chapter One. Violence and Intimacy as Entertainment   13
    Human Dignity Needs the Media
    Changes in the Public Structure
    The Triumphal March of the Market Principle
    The Media and the Taste for Violence
    The Role of Ethics
    Responsibility for One's Own Actions
    Principles for a Universalist Ethic
    Television and the Ban on Images

Chapter Two. Taking Liberties with Human Dignity:
    The Example of Sports   31
    The Meaning of Sport
    Principles of Sports
    Effects of Social Change
    Ethic of Dignity or Ethic of Interests

The Olympic Model or the Jesus Model
Achievement and Success
Sports and Value of Nature
Individuality and Sociability

Chapter Three. The Society of the Majority and the
    Minorities: Conditions of Living Together   51
    Internal Diversity and External Boundaries
    Majorities and Minorities
    Multiculturalism
    Acknowledging the Stranger and One's Own Identity
    The Offer of Successful Multiculturalism
    Coexistence in Cultural Diversity

Chapter Four. A Look Back at the Gulf War   75
    May War Be God's Will?
    Is There Such a Thing as Inevitable War?
    Are There Worse Things than War?
    What Is the Role of Religion?
    Opposing Options in the Issue of War and Peace
    The Gulf War and Religion's Loss of Credibility

Chapter Five. Military Violence after the Cold War   97
    Ethical Principles of Peace
    Peacekeeping Duties of the Community of Nations
    Peacekeeping Missions
    Combat Missions
    The Balkan War and Military Intervention
    Summary

Chapter Six. Violence against Humanity and Nature:
    The Necessity for a Planetary Ethos   113
    Human Dignity in Antiquity and in the
       Christian Tradition
    The New Turn toward Human Dignity
    The Transition to Human Rights
    Accessibility to Reasons and the Power to Bind
    Ethics, Responsibility, Power
    The Concept of Power

Minimizing Violence
Power and Violence
Planetary Ethos
"Project World Ethos"
Human Rights and Planetary Ethos
Ethical Dimensions of Human Rights
Third Generation of Human Rights
The Rights of Nature
Relative Universalism

Notes   151

Index   155

Foreword

Daniel Berrigan, S.J.

To put matters plainly from the start, *Violence* is a work of extraordinary merit. Such a claim immediately invites attention to the signs of the times. Which is to say, the "Olympic model" of life in American culture (as in German or, for that matter, any contemporary culture of the so-called advanced societies) all but cancels out the "Jesus model" proposed by the author as a saving alternative. (The latter, alas, is already obscured or downright violated by the churches.) Greed races fast; the golden calf has grown monstrously into a mighty, bullish, world-encompassing market.

Our world, in sum, is a public spectacle of brutish economics, military muscle, and governments in servitude to mammon and its godlings.

But the large picture, the terrain of the public intellectual, is hardly the whole picture. We do have ethicians of the quality of Wolfgang Huber. Their task is a saving one; to me it recalls a scene in the Book of Daniel.

There we are told that a king and his henchmen are seated at a banquet. In a moment of absolute irresponsibility, the king calls for the sacred vessels, loot of the Temple of Jerusalem. The guests raise the chalices to their gods.

And out of nowhere a hand appears and traces words on the wall. From stupor to terror—the rakes' progress.

Daniel is summoned. He translates the words; they are pure judgment.

Evidently the blasphemous orgy is meant to stand surrogate for a larger social scene. The banqueters are actors in a cannibal culture. They are the ultimate consumers; they eat and drink the flesh and blood of the victims—specifically the exiles and slaves, Daniel's people.

Shortly, the prophet issues an ethical summons. His words are, in the closest sense, prophetic, a revelation, an epiphany, in two stages.

First, the cultural analysis of things as they are: the orgy as evidence of cultural anomie, appetite and greed on rampage.

Then, the judgment: here, now, the human vocation is violated and scorned, along with creation itself.

I received recently an invitation reminiscent of the imperial orgy. A spiffy brochure arrived in the mail. It offered in Atlanta a king's ransom of Olympic perquisites (for a price, of course, but that was cannily tucked away on the last page). The perks—a mansion all to myself, a stretch limousine to convey me about, front seats at every athletic event, a week of menus fit to give one the blind staggers.

All this and more for $50,000, one-fifth of which, due in advance, would guarantee my place at this preadolescent feeding frenzy.

The "Olympic model" indeed; it is "competition" with a vengeance, as Huber's metaphor indicates, and the "runaway market economy."

If reservations occur to me concerning this important book, they center around Huber's lengthy discussion of the just-war theory. Is it expedient or profitable once more to review the squalid pseudo-religious rhetoric and mutual demonizing of Messrs. Hussein and Bush?

Immediately after the Gulf slaughter, an editorial appeared in the Italian Jesuit publication, *Civilta Catolica*. It declared that the war, waged with modern "conventional" weapons, was an exercise in indiscriminate horror. It had at least this sorry merit: it buried once for all, any possible appeal in modern warfare to the just-war theory.

For the distinguished, courageous author, one suggestion. Let the just-war theory, along with hoary justifications of slavery, capital punishment, abortion, and other assorted grotesqueries, be granted, at long last, Christian burial.

Preface to the
American Edition

Human violence against other humans is the most disturbing and most challenging problem facing the world today. The struggle for life in the slums of Rio de Janeiro or Calcutta, ethnic problems in parts of South Africa or in Bosnia, class-related tensions in the United States or in Europe, xenophobic attacks against refugees in Germany, sexual mistreatment and child abuse all over the world—these and other phenomena demonstrate that violence permeates our societies, and, indeed, our whole life.

Whoever switches on television programs or looks at movie or video advertising will quickly realize that we are confronted with a new "culture of violence." Violence, even in its most sadistic, dehumanizing forms, is openly shown and used as a means of so-called entertainment. Many indicators suggest that the uninhibited presentation of violence in the media contributes remarkably to a preparedness to use violence in real life. An education in media consumption is as necessary as an ethics of media production.

American society, in this as in many other respects, is the forerunner of other societies in our world. The present stage of American society anticipates the future of other societies. America is the place in our world where a specific sensitivity to new dimensions of violence first emerges—for example, the specific awareness of youth violence, racial violence, sexual or familial abuse, and violence in gender relations. But American tradition also incorporates decisive instances of a "culture of nonviolence." American independence began with a new understanding of human dignity and human rights. Civil courage and civil disobedience as elements of a mature political culture were first formulated by an American, Henry David Thoreau. The nonviolent struggle for civil rights found its decisive success in America, specifically in the work and words of Martin Luther King, Jr. I am deeply convinced that the time is ripe to mobilize those traditions and to confront the omnipresent "culture of violence" with the strength of this "culture of nonviolence."

What we need is a new and broad public debate on such issues on a clear ethical basis. Through this book I hope to clarify what an ethics of human dignity can contribute to this debate, in particular the potential within Jewish and Christian traditions for an adequate approach to this topic.

I have attempted to analyze the mechanisms of violence in different areas of the social and political arena, such as sports, media, the multiethnic and multicultural reality of our societies, the new emergence of military violence in international relations, and the violent attitude of humans to nonhuman nature. Such examples need concreteness and contextuality. My present context is Europe after the end of the Cold War, Germany after the fall of the Berlin Wall. But the problem I am dealing with is not restricted to this context; it is global. In Europe and America we have more in common than some people realize. Together we should try to drive to the root of the dangers with which our society is confronted. What we need in these days is more globality and therefore more intercontextuality in our ethical reflection. What I present in this book is a contribution to the global ethos for which we are searching.

I deeply appreciate the efforts of Fortress Press in preparing this American edition. Especially I thank Michael West for his help as senior editor and Ruth C. L. Gritsch for her translation. I am personally indebted to Daniel Berrigan, S. J., for honoring me and my work with his Foreword to this book.

Berlin, Easter 1996   *Wolfgang Huber*

INTRODUCTION

Our Daily Violence

It is Friday afternoon, February 12, 1993, in Liverpool, England. Denise Bulger is shopping for weekend provisions in the New Strand Mall, accompanied by her two-year-old son James and her friend Nicola Baily. During just one moment of inattention, James is torn away from his mother by two ten-year-old boys, who are seen heading in the direction of the city. Two days later, James's mangled body is found on the railroad tracks, dead from the severe injuries inflicted on him by his two kidnappers before the train hit him. People asked the question, Had the two ten-year-old Liverpool boys wished to try out what they had seen innumerable times on television, or in films and videos?

Soon afterward, a television drama based on this event was shown to the largest viewing audience ever in England.

This murder of a child committed by children gave rise to a call for more violence. An angry mob, assembling with the intention of taking justice into their own hands, attempted to stop a police car transporting the two suspects. The kidnapping and murder of James Bulger—as well as many of the reactions to the event—have become a *bona fide* warning of the brutalization that engulfs us all if we allow acts of violence and depictions of violence to proceed unhindered.

FORMS OF VIOLENCE

Not a day goes by that does not bring the news of violence into our living rooms. Nor does a day pass when we do not see and experience violence in our immediate vicinity, even when we try to shut our eyes to it. Each day we receive reports from the various war fronts of the world, but this violence does not cease when the public has lost interest. Moreover, we consume a tremendous amount of violence through the entertainment programs we watch every day on television. How these shows affect the behavior and the souls of children and even of adults is not yet fully understood. Violence surrounds us every day in our families, in the schoolyard, on public transportation, even on the highways. And every day we ourselves participate in this violence—at least in those acts of violence that affect nature and the matrix of natural life.

Nothing today renders the search for sound ethical guidance more acute than this outbreak of violence in its various forms. Vandalism and violence are increasing in our schools, as well as the sadism linked to these occurrences. In the past, fist fights in the schoolyard during recess ended when the victim was knocked to the ground; today the victim receives a gratuitous kick in the face as well—or is stabbed or shot.

Only recently has discussion about sexual abuse of women and children become public, but there are still many places it is not mentioned. Most of the time, such abuse is committed in secret, yet the number of unreported cases must be very large. There is a growing demand for women's and children's shelters, in which the victims can at least be protected temporarily from the violence that threatens them.

A growing number of older people are afraid of being attacked in their own homes or on the street. They stream in large numbers to public meetings on how to protect themselves.

Contemporary critics blame the media above all for this increase in violence. Videos and television programs that without compunction depict acts of violence are offered and consumed in massive numbers. The overflowing reports of felonies, hunger, and war in the daily news arouse a sense of helplessness and lead to resignation in many people. But, for many young people who lack the inhibitions that would prevent them from giving free rein to their violent tendencies, these reports may also arouse a readiness to imitate what they see.

But there is no reason to consider this new readiness to become violent as a phenomenon confined to the young. Tourists to Germany, for instance, are increasingly frightened by the aggressiveness with which Germans race on the autobahn, caring neither for the environment nor for their fellow humans. This kind of violent act is generally considered to be merely a lapse in good manners and, despite the shocking number of accident victims, it is, for the most part, seen as innocuous. Many people try to suppress the awareness of how this behavior on the roads and this wasting of energy violate nature.

More depressing are the hatred and violence directed against foreigners, immigrants, and minorities. Although the German situation is hardly unique and can be compared in many respects to other European or American situations, it is instructive. These acts are in large measure the work of the extreme right. In 1991, the German parliament released a list citing 3,535 criminal acts of violence and attacks on foreigners committed by rightwing extremists. By 1992, the number had doubled to 7,195. Seventeen people, including seven foreigners, were killed in Germany in 1992 through rightwing-extremist violence.

The increase in anti-Semitic outrages is particularly shaming in light of German history. There were 77 cases reported in 1992 of vandalism in Jewish cemeteries, monuments, and other Jewish community buildings. Crude, unadulterated anti-Semitism is spreading simultaneously with attacks on refugees.

Meanwhile, the brutality directed against foreign residents is spreading to other minorities. Persons with disabilities and those who assist them—for example, bus drivers or train conductors—are publicly insulted and mistreated in the midst of crowded railroad stations or city squares, while most passersby look away.

Not just right-wing extremist ideologies are used as rational-izations for aggression, but the right-wing violence in Germany at this time is particularly alarming. Groups of five to six thousand skinheads ready to use violence have been organized, half in Eastern Germany and half in the West.

The age of those committing these acts of violence is worri-some. More than two-thirds of those accused of committing offenses against foreign residents are under the age of twenty; the rest are, almost without exception, between twenty-one and thirty years old. Only a small number of such extremist offend-ers are older than thirty. Yet it would be a mistake to expect extreme rightist views to be confined to the younger genera-tion. Nationalistic attitudes can be found among older Germans as well; even if these views are not expressed in open violence, they are nevertheless demonstrated by loud applause or quiet nods of approval.

Xenophobia and anti-Semitism are not confined to Ger-many; similar examples occur in other European countries. These outrages have justifiably been abhorred throughout the world. Yet it cannot be denied that the readiness to use vio-lence has spread with frightening rapidity through all of Ger-many. The horrifying climax came on November 23, 1992, when three Turkish women—Bahide Arslan, Yelzin Arslan, and Asye Yilmaz—were burned to death in Mölln, victims of arson. Only at that point did many people realize that these acts of aggres-sion against foreign residents could also be committed against other minorities. Even when only a small minority is committed to the use of violence and ruthless criminality, it does so in a favorable environment. Social indifference predominates, and the protective spirit of practical solidarity is rare.

"Chains of light" were organized to reanimate this spirit. During the autumn of 1992, many Germans took part in dem-onstrations for the first time in their lives, sensing that the be-ginnings of violence must be opposed. They asked themselves if it were not perhaps too late already. But they discovered that human dignity is indivisible. Many suddenly became aware that this spreading violence must be confronted with a clear confession of the universal dignity of all human beings.

But chains of light are not enough. Long-term solutions are needed, which demand civil courage, political straight thinking, and a sense of realism. Immigrants will not cease arriving in the United States, and refugees will keep coming to Western Europe, at least as long as the East European and Third World nations do not succeed in effectively stemming the causes of flight. The difficulties that inevitably occur with the influx of refugees, and the disappointments that unfailingly accompany the efforts to integrate foreigners must not lead us to reserve human dignity to the native-born and to deny it to the refugees. The test of a society is how it deals with its refugees.

The problem of violence has been unexpectedly exacerbated by the collapse of the centralized economies in Eastern Europe and the disintegration of the Soviet Empire. These factors put an end to dictatorships, yet also created a vacuum into which streamed long-outdated claims to power, nationalistic yearnings, and even illusions of ethnic homogeneity in a particular territory. The splitting of Yugoslavia led to the escalation of atrocities and war. "Ethnic cleansing," rape camps, people subjected to hunger, cold, sickness, and death, have all demonstrated that humans are capable of frightful acts of violence. The perpetrators are even more ready to commit these acts if they believe they are obeying their political or military superiors and serving a greater cause.

Horrible events like these have reawakened the pessimistic views of humankind, advanced by some behaviorist psychologists, that humans are animals who have lost their natural inhibitions, and whose yearning for security and happiness does not hinder them from reaching for violence first whenever problems mount. Such an assessment simply dissolves the ambivalence in human behavior in favor of a negative evaluation. This kind of thinking links the negative evaluation of humans to an optimistic view of military effectiveness. Confidence in the military's ability to solve political problems by means of violence has grown to an astonishing degree. Many people believe that massive violations of human rights, such as those occurring in the Balkan states, can only be corrected through military intervention. But they have no answer for the doubts whether intervention really would break the chain of violence or merely add links to it.

To be sure, it is necessary to determine once again the duties of the military, especially in light of the international unrest following the end of the Cold War. Many people urge expanding the scope of the armed forces' duties in general. Others concentrate on demanding that the necessary instruments for military interventions be put at the disposal of the United Nations. Many view war as a continuation of politics by other means. They maintain that the peace-oriented ethical insights developed at the time of the Cold War—above all, but not solely, by the churches and peace movements—are outdated. Others warn against gambling away the chances of disarmament that resulted from the end of the Cold War. Once again, we question whether human dignity can possibly be, or indeed must be, defended through the use of force.

Are we still capable of digesting all that we experience and receive through the media? Are we able to win out over omnipresent violence? Does the lifestyle of a society that emits this kind of potential violence have any future at all? These questions become even more unavoidable when posed in circumstances characterized by profound historical changes. At the end of the Cold War, people in the United States experienced the consequences of a profound economic shift, while Europe experienced deep and dramatic changes unlike any since World War II. The related loss of a sense of direction not only stamps national politics but also the everyday life of every individual. All issues are influenced by this upheaval, even the question of our ethical orientation amidst daily violence.

RESPONSIBLE LIFESTYLES

The scene has changed. A few years ago, the contrast between East and West, between Western democracies and Eastern countries ruled by state-socialism, provided the parameters within which the people could find their direction, in both small and large issues. Over the course of forty years, the East and West developed different lifestyles, and, with the collapse of state socialism, each was ready with different answers to the important questions of life, ranging from family planning to funeral practices. Now, in a new context, Europe and the United States are confronted with the question of which sources will give them strength, which traditions will shape them, which future they will choose. Other parts of the world are watching keenly to see which answers we will give to these questions. After all, we live in mutual dependence within this one world.

This challenge can perhaps be postponed for a time by referring to the fact that the collapse of Communist East and Central Europe has proven the superiority of the free market economy and of democracy. But that comparison alone will not be a convincing answer in the long run. It will be necessary to arrive at an understanding about the substance of our life. Moreover, we must take into consideration our great variety of traditions and lifestyles while, at the same time, we search for their unifying factors.

This new challenge hits us at the end of an epoch characterized by an unforeseen individualization of lifestyles. As the possibilities of choice increased in the 1980s, the West in particular was shaped by a lessening of ties between institutions and lifestyles. It is true that a large number of people did not profit from this increased freedom: The unemployed, the refugees, single people, and the aged were all losers in this "social progress." But others found the possibilities of determining their own ways of living raised to a degree undreamed of a few decades ago. Flexible work hours and the great variety of possible vocations are examples of this.

But the step from increased freedom to "anything goes" is a small one. Many consider the "community of experience" to be simply a "market of options" in which they can choose whatever suits them without having to accept responsibility for it—whether it is a matter of dress or travel, of forms of partnership or careers.

No matter how valuable growth in individual liberty is, it can become problematic when the sense of solidarity that considers the liberty of the other as important as one's own is eroded. As enriching as individual free choice can be, it can also become dubious if a growing number of people are overtaxed by it. Only those who are sufficiently sure of their own identity can use individual freedom responsibly. How can people who lack important means of establishing an identity of their own form their individuality? The growing predilection for violence among young people reflects our increasing loss of direction in a world of individualistic lifestyle options.

At the same time, there is the question of how much further individual claims to personal freedom—thus the erosion of solidarity—can be pushed. The crisis in Germany brought about by unification, like the social dislocation in the United States brought about by economic change, contains the hidden question: What way of life will prove durable and responsible? For what living conditions can we in the long run be responsible, not only economically, but also ecologically and socially? What form of living together conforms to our concept of humanity?

THE PROCESS OF CLARIFICATION

The social, cultural, economic, and media developments of recent years, we have seen, have bestowed an unexpected and depressing relevance to our search for the ethical substance of our way of life. Even a few years ago, no one would have predicted that the search for the relationship of violence to human dignity would gain such intensity and become the key issue of ethical position, which will occupy us for many years. Clarifications are necessary, in view of the various levels of human association.

As regards the relationship between violence and human dignity, there are varied models of living together such as: family and school, ethnic communities, watching television, and participating in sports. Moreover, involvement in larger geopolitical issues—such as intervening in civil wars or resolving international conflicts—presupposes the answer to the question of whether the use of violence always contradicts human dignity or whether it can, in an extreme emergency, be employed in the service of humanity.

Some of these questions will be taken up and—as far as possible—clarified in this book. The chapters originated in various settings, and I have discussed the ideas in this book with many people. Although my answers must remain provisional and fragmentary, their starting point is certainly unambiguous: the conviction that the character of human dignity is inalienable and indivisible. The only way we can confront increasingly widespread violence is if we once again become aware of our responsibility to the dignity shared by all human beings.

For Christians, the confession of the dignity and value of human beings is anchored in the insight that all human beings are created in the image of God. The Enlightenment tradition renewed this concept of human dignity by considering rational human beings as those who must never be used simply as means toward an end, but must rather be acknowledged as ends in themselves. The significance of human dignity was again recognized in the twentieth century, when efforts were made to obtain worldwide acknowledgment of human rights.

The massive violation of elementary dictates of humanity on the part of totalitarian and authoritarian regimes meant that human rights became the central theme of legal developments, political action, and ethical orientation. When giving reasons for this new orientation, contemporary documents on human rights and constitutional rights refer regularly to the secure and inalienable dignity of humankind.

The Preamble to the General Declaration of Human Rights of December 10, 1948, for example, points to the "Recognition of all members of the human family in their inherent dignity and their equally inalienable rights" as "the basis of freedom, justice, and peace in the world." Article I starts with the affirmation that "all humans are born free and of equal value. They are endowed with reason and conscience and should encounter each other in the spirit of brotherhood."

The Bonn Constitution of 1949 links human value and human rights in a remarkable way, by explaining in Article I that "The dignity of a human being is inalienable. To honor it and protect it is the duty of every government authority."

The concept of human dignity is among the most controversial in the language of ethics and politics. Yet those whose dignity has been disregarded or even trampled on know full well what human dignity means. Its meaning is established by the denial of it. Human dignity attains an indisputable obviousness from the massive governmental attacks on the life, liberty, and integrity of innumerable human beings.

Human dignity must retain its validity without exception. Nor can it be revoked from a single human being. The mentally or physically handicapped, criminals, the unborn, even the dead—all have a right to this dignity.

Governmental authorities are the first to be placed under obligation to provide the human rights based on this human dignity. But human dignity is the decisive criterion not only for governmental action; it also forms the basis for all other forms of human interaction, having immediate ethical implications. Wherever human dignity is denied, it destroys not only the legitimacy of governmental behavior but also the humaneness of social intercourse as a whole. It happens not only when terrorist regimes make intentional use of violence and disregard human freedom, but also whenever individuals or social groups employ violence, idealize it, or make it seem harmless.

That is why a society's humane quality is at stake when exhibition of violence grows without hindrance. Humanity is in peril when the dignity of foreigners and minorities is defamed or injured. Any attempt to protect human rights by governmental means is doomed to fail in a society that has forgotten how to respect human dignity.

Clear and unequivocal government intervention is required when human dignity is under violent attack. But more than the necessary means of police and judicial authority should be invoked. Government policies oriented to the equal dignity of all human beings should confront the spirit that stamps minorities as second-class persons. But more than government action is required; the indifference to human dignity and the rights of others must be overcome in families, in churches, in the media, in schools, and in science and medicine. All who wish to safeguard their own dignity and liberty in the long run must do so in ways that account for the dignity and liberty of others. It is high time for society to learn once again the relationship between one's own dignity and that of others, between one's own liberty and that of others. Individuals are just as responsible for doing this as are all the institutions that participate in the advancement of knowledge and consciousness.

CHAPTER ONE

Violence and Intimacy as Entertainment

As American viewers of the O. J. Simpson trial or reports of the Oklahoma City federal building bombing can testify, more than fictional drama fills television nowadays. Recently in Germany, for instance, a hostage drama and a mine accident kept the television and tabloid reporters in a state of breathlessness. They left few measures untried in their attempt to get sensational pictures. Their utter lack of scruples at the mine accident upset me even more than their lust for sensationalism during the hostage drama. As one source reported, "The journalists disguised themselves as doctors and fire fighters in order to sneak into the waiting room where the families, in care of a pastor, spent the night between hope and fear."[1] Photographers went so far as to climb the walls of buildings and shoot their pictures through bathroom windows, subjecting the six rescued miners to "downright harassment and persecution." Some members of the press made every effort to push their way into the hospital in front of the survivors.

Ironically, no one might have been rescued if it had not been for the television directional microphone, which had been placed in the mine for other reasons. It was supposed to make the gasps of suffocating miners audible in viewers' living rooms. Had the Moloch of entertainment pushed aside the last ethical barriers?

Media ethics are still in their infancy. Theologians as well as philosophers have treated the subject shabbily. Yet it is undoubtedly a pressing issue, and it involves much more than simply an ethic of journalism. It calls for an ethic not only of media producers but also of media consumers. The issue is so urgent because the media do so much to shape sense of reality. We live in a mediated reality. Our image of reality is formed more sharply through the media than through our direct unfiltered experience.

This mediated reality is a mark of advanced industrialized societies, where everyone lives in this artificially produced environment: politicians, actors, journalistic interpreters, heroes of the corner bar, old people, preschool children. In the process, particular preconceptions are solidified regarding what determines reality and what is of decisive importance within it. These preconceptions then guide our choices of news reporting and entertainment in a kind of continuous feedback. Moreover, they also affect how we shape our lives and how we deal with other people or things.

Television affects our daily life more than any other medium. It determines the day's routine for many families and many single people. It brings the outside world into our private realm with a plethora of information and entertainment. The more competition determines television's program offerings, the greater the pressure to make the programs entertaining.

In the ratings war, news must be handled like entertainment. Two themes in entertainment programs—but often in news programs as well—gain obvious prominence: first is a daily dose of death as an essential part of the evening's entertainment. The presentation of acts of violence and catastrophes enjoys high ratings. Second is the erotic image as an essential part of the evening's entertainment. Even public television sells the erotic image in order to remain competitive. The themes are often combined, and violence in sex is particularly attractive. This mix of violence and intimacy is offered as entertainment to the media-watching society—via video films, magazines, and tabloids as well as television—to the degree that they promise higher shares of the market.

To try to solve this problem solely by prohibiting such displays of sex and violence would be näive. Yet one cannot avoid the question, What limits of the permissible must be set by legal means? One must be clear, moreover, on the criteria used to judge the public presentation of violence and eroticism.

The answer most often given by producers is an economic one. Their criterion is acceptance by the market, as measured by ratings. Another answer, increasingly rare, is an aesthetic one, directed to the *quality* of the depictions of violence or intimacy. Rarest are the answers based on ethics, since the media increasingly believe that there is no room for ethical considerations where the market rules. Commercial television stations present this view without hesitation; public stations at least still exhibit pangs of conscience, even though one gets the impression that they too are increasingly driven by higher ratings.

I, on the other hand, start with the presupposition that all media must let themselves be measured by ethical standards, not only in their news broadcasts but also in their entertainment programs. Since they occupy key positions in society by transmiting the news and shaping attitudes and behavior, they should behave responsibly.

This applies especially to public radio and television networks, particularly those in the European states, because their status is based on the insight that the media possess a decisive power to influence the interpretation of events which guides the behavior of citizens. Public radio and television networks are therefore legally obligated to justify the criteria they use to determine the contents of their programs. Their public status would have lost its legitimacy if competition for the market had become their standard for programming. However, the present problem of media ethics would not be solved with responsible programming on the part of public stations alone.

HUMAN DIGNITY NEEDS THE MEDIA

The concept of human dignity merits a key position in public ethics and has guiding force for media ethics as well. I will make a detour to explain this.

In the year 1795, Immanuel Kant published his proposal "To Eternal Peace," wherein he named three conditions for a permanent peace between nations. First is a republican constitution in which all citizens enjoy freedom and equality and are dependent on only those laws applicable to all. The second condition is international law by a league of free nations. The final condition is worldwide civil rights, guaranteeing every human being a secure life in every nation. But Kant added this statement to his vision of universal civil rights:

> Since the prevalent extensive community of the peoples of the earth has now progressed so far that the violation of the law in *one* place on earth is felt in *all* places, the idea of a universal civil rights is not a fantastic or exaggerated kind of vision of law; rather it is a necessary complement to the unwritten code of national as well as civil law and to civil human rights as a whole, and thus to eternal peace, which one can boast of approaching only under these conditions.[2]

The decisive factor in Kant's vision is the presupposition to which he ties a functioning universal civil law and so a durable peace: that is, a community of human beings so strong that a violation of law in one place on earth can be perceived everywhere. The world was further removed from such a community in 1795 than the philosopher of Königsberg wished to acknowledge. Nor have we attained it today by a long shot. But we do have realistic reasons to hope and to work for it.

Such a community would not be one of universal empathy. It would not achieve reality just because love of neighbor is being proclaimed. Rather, it would depend on structural preconditions. One can only talk of such a community if the news of a violation of rights in one place is reported in all other places. Consequently, a worldwide community of law presupposes worldwide media communication. Universal human rights can be conceived of only when violations of human rights can be noted throughout the world. Human dignity is dependent on the media, for the media can report the suffering intentionally imposed on human beings.

The intentions and goals with which acts of violence are reported are of critical importance. It really is not the task of television to satisfy the need for entertainment of a person presumably dependent on a daily diet of violence to sate his or her aggressive drives. The media's ethically legitimate task is rather to contribute to the overcoming of such violence. Their obligation is to report the intentional violence to which people are subjected in such a way that these violations of rights are felt everywhere and awaken people's readiness to defend respect for human integrity.

For the media, distinguishing between contradictory aims when depicting violence is an ethical necessity. No doubt one presentation of violence—seen from a valid and perhaps even necessary viewpoint—can double the attack on human dignity by making a stranger's suffering and pain the means to satisfy the lust for sensationalism and the subject of voyeurism. This kind of reporting then panders to the public's demand for entertainment or the satisfaction of their aggressive drives. As a result, the media not only violates the victim's dignity but also blunts ethical sensitivity regarding violence. Even when the line between such manipulation of violence and the necessary reporting of violence is not easy to distinguish, that distinction remains crucial.

The kind of presentation of violence to which the media are ethically obligated has as its criterion respect for a human being's dignity and rights. The political barbarism of our century made the proclamation of universal human rights necessary, but it made sense only on the basis of the present state of media development. It is the ongoing duty of the media to see to it that it continues to make sense.

In Germany, for example, the Bonn constitution linked up with this proclamation of universally valid human rights, and this proclamation was also the basis on which the German national press and media networks were established. This was a demanding concept of a free medium committed to human dignity. To an unusual degree both legislation and juridical processes in the Federal Republic of Germany safeguarded the freedom of the press—a freedom that is not just a product of the free market justifying almost anything, but one that established the conditions necessary to guarantee the ability of the press to do justice to its commitment to the dignity of human beings. Otto B. Roegele derived the following consequences from the formulation:

> If constitutional law places the dignity of humans at the head of its constitutions, everything else can only be of lesser importance: business interests as well as the public's curiosity; the ambition of a clever reporter as well as goals of political propaganda. Only in the rare cases of a collision between the public's right to know (for example, the sudden incapacity of a minister to hold office) and privacy may a journalist transgress the line—of course at the risk of being sued.[3]

Those were still idyllic notions of what kind of collisions journalists could encounter, today's colleagues would add.

CHANGES IN THE PUBLIC STRUCTURE

In 1962, when Jürgen Habermas described "the change in public structure," he was thinking of the state-socialistic transformation of the middle class. After more than three decades, it is time to update the change in public structures. The separation between society as the sphere of private interests and the state as the site of public affairs no longer functions. Organized into groups and alliances, private interests conquer the public realm. The media now serve advertisers and public relations.

Neil Postman provided noteworthy stimulus in his analysis of the American development. I will take up his thesis with my own variations.

There are different structures in the public realm along with different forms of communication. An *oral* culture learns about reality by way of listening to stories. Experiences are told in tales in which the listeners can participate. A culture of oral tradition is ruled by the public form of storytelling.

A culture determined by the *written* word separates fact from fiction. It demands that its readers test the truth of a report and the accuracy of an argument. A culture of the written word is ruled by the public form of argument.

But an *image-based* culture, determined by moving pictures, allows fact to blend with fiction. Viewers are entertained with real or invented events, with staged reality or staged theater. The culture of television is ruled by the public form of entertainment. That is, the *entertainment* value of what is presented takes precedence over its *information* value. The viewers' readiness to accept what they see is more important than their critical review of what they see.

Television invests what it creates with the urgency of the factual. The kidnapper or bandit really dies in a hail of bullets— and does so in my living room. But television also invests reality with the entertainment value of fiction, for even death must be entertaining. The new trend toward "reality TV," seen in staged re-enactments of actual events, expresses it very well. Nothing is as entertaining as the immediacy of reality. "Reality TV" acts like a powerful magnet attracting viewers to a private television viewing of accidents and kidnapping, theft and murder, suffering and despair. Reality is turned on as entertainment. Turned off is the readiness to help shape this reality responsibly.

The boundary between reality and fiction disappears with the predominance of entertainment. Hotels, restaurants, theme parks, and entertainment centers spring up in imitation of the settings depicted in film or on television. Further, there is great entertainment value not only in staged violence but also in real violence. If the camera catches a view of real hostage takers on the screen, there is only one thing to do: keep them on camera even if that hinders the rescue of the hostages.

One "must" follow up with pictures and interviews, for they are "news"—but what is *not* news from this point of view? Catastrophes and acts of violence receive wide coverage not because viewers are thereby empowered to take a position regarding ambivalent reality, but because violence is a successful means of entertainment. Violence is also given a lot of time in news broadcasts, because news must be entertaining too.

Violence as a means of entertainment, I am convinced, explains in large part the growing lack of inhibition with which images of violent acts are pursued and broadcast. To this is linked another tendency, namely to use intimacy as an instrument of public entertainment. There is no room left for a separation of private from public in the culture of entertainment.

Granted, the positive aspects of the media's presentation of human sexuality must be acknowledged. The erotic image is not a modern invention of the media. Ancient sculpture and Raphael's larger-than-life paintings are sufficient proof of that. The beauty of a human body can become a reflection of human dignity; first the arts, and later the media, worked against making human sexuality taboo. In that sense, they contributed to seeing the totality of humanity.

There is a sharp line, even if not always easy to draw, between the portrayal of sexuality in the service of the total image of humans and the sale of human sexuality as a commodity. Far beyond this line are the numerous films, videos, and television programs in which sadistic violence in sexual acts is depicted, as well as programs that make television viewers voyeuristic participants in the intimacy of others. A ban on graphic depictions of violence should, in such cases, be enforced without exception—and certainly not limited just to television programs aired before 11:00 P.M.

The line between public and private is blurred not only where human sexuality has been made into marketable entertainment. This boundary is also transgressed wherever the media shove and push to obtain access to the suffering and grief of people. Ada Brandes, for example, reported[4] what happened to the wife of a television talk-show host before and after his death. Reporters not only made constant telephone calls but they also kept a callous siege on her home both day and night, agreeing to depart only if they received family photographs— all of this during the vigil for the dying and grief for the dead. Ada Brandes comments:

> Then the survivors of the mining accident in Borken are literally assaulted; the children of the murdered diplomat von Braun-mühl are harassed and hassled in school; reporters jostle and shove at grave side—the greater the suffering, the better for business. Human interest must make it into print even when it was obtained by inhuman means, even if it saps the last vestige of strength from the subjects of the story.[5]

THE TRIUMPHAL MARCH OF THE MARKET PRINCIPLE

How can one explain the fact that the media's obsession with intimacy does not even shrink from flaunting suffering and the pain of death? Of course this unscrupulousness has an individual aspect, but I do not want to describe or analyze that at this point. More important is, without a doubt, the structural connection to which this kind of unscrupulous pursuit of pictures gives rise. For—note well—the issue is obtaining pictures that do not contain new information but instead increase the so-called entertainment value of already reported news, such as, for example, the death of a well known talk-show host.

This lack of scruples can only be explained by the triumphal march of the market principle into the media. The transformation in the structure of the public sphere that we are experiencing is substantially determined by the altered function awarded to competition for this public. In the early years after World War II, competition was understood as an instrument of social control, as something that facilitated a better allocation of resources than would a centrally administered plan. Theoreticians of a social market economy emphasized that the governing principles of such an economy are solidarity and justice, not competition as an instrument of control.

Today we consider phrases like these ideologically suspect and have no significance in our present social reality. For "modern" society, competition is no longer an instrument of control, but a principle of structure. Nowhere is this as clearly demonstrated as in the realm of the media. The proliferation of commercial and cable networks has accelerated the process, resulting in a self-commercialization of public broadcasting networks.

One critic has declared that—besides paralysis incurred through bureaucratic agencies, adaptations made because of worries about survival, personal political stinginess and direct political intervention in programming—self-commercialization is one of the great factors in the erosion of the public broadcasting system. He spoke of "capitulation to the ratings" and their "almost panic-stricken anticipatory adaptation of programs to the feared attractive popular offerings of the new commercial networks." [6]

My diagnosis is that the oral culture as well as the culture of the written word still exist, but they are being overtaken by the culture of moving pictures. Personal experiences and discursive arguments are losing their significance—entertainment is winning out. In entertainment, fact and fiction are blurring; violence has as much entertainment value as sexuality; privacy is turned into an instrument providing public amusement. The "normal catastrophes" of modern society are just good enough to provide entertainment—an airplane crash at an air show, a grisly double murder in Los Angeles, a mine disaster, a terrorist bombing in Oklahoma, the killing of a person at the hands of hostage-taking gangsters, the crash of a hijacked airliner over Lockerbie, or just the death of a talk-show host. Human beings have become merely raw material for stories with a "human touch." This "human touch," however, is a long way from being humane.

THE MEDIA AND THE TASTE FOR VIOLENCE

The increase in media presentations of violence is even more disquieting because in real life the taste for violence in our society is growing. To make direct causative links would be premature, it would add to the confusion, as well as be innocuous, to simply blame the media for new forms of violence in the schools or for right-wing extremist cruelties against foreigners, migrants, or minorities. Not only the change in the media, but the shifts in the social climate as a whole find their expression in these new types of violent phenomena.

Why do children exhibit a new taste for violence—indeed, sometimes for a sadistic cruelty that can no longer be compared in any way to the playground fights of the past? One critic has observed a decided shift of conscience in many young people.[7] The categories of strong and weak have taken the place of the basic categories of good and evil. Strength counts as good and is shown outwardly. Weakness is counted as bad and is mocked and even persecuted. The weak are humiliated so as to make the strong more certain of their strength. Of course, that the strong depend on violently humiliating the weak points to a deep-seated lack of direction on the part of the strong. Between the challenge to choose a life-style of one's own from the great variety of possible options, and the lack of perspective in one's personal life, one's family, or one's school situation, a vacuum is created in which the tendency toward violence can spread.

Exhibitions of strength and brutality toward the weak make it possible for the individual who suffers from a shortage of direction and hope to find a place among the strong. That explains the individual style, the ideology, and the behavior of many skinheads, for example. It is not coincidental that their acts of violence are directed not just against foreigners but also against the handicapped and those who show solidarity with the weak.

To blame the media alone for the violence in the schools or the brutality of some youth would indeed be short-sighted. And yet there can be no doubt that a certain exchange of attitudes confirming each other is operating here. The substantial and increasing depiction of violence in the media disarms the viewers' moral repulsion against violence, and not only raises their willingness to accept violence as inevitable, but also raises their desire to take part in it.

On the other hand, a social climate that considers the strong good and the weak evil strengthens and enforces those forms of entertainment that demonstrate the superiority of the strong. This kind of atmosphere contributes to raising the ratings of shows that depict violence. Thus producers who want to keep up their share of the market think they cannot refuse to present violence in their programs. The media presentations of violence, however, do not lessen but instead increase society's taste for violence.

To what extent can actual violence be found acceptable? Even if we cannot blame the media as the direct cause of society's predilection for violence, neither can they deny their partial responsibility. Consequently, they must analyze their own role more thoroughly and critically than they have done, and act according to the conclusions they draw from the insights thus gained.

The media's role is rendered innocuous when public relations professionals differentiate between the presentation of "intentional" violence and that of "unintentional violence." [8] "Intentional violence" is the willful damage of persons or things. "Unintentional" violence is damage caused by accidents, catastrophes, or similar events. On the basis of this differentiation, he concludes that the depiction of unintentional violence is less harmful than that of intentional violence when judged by media ethics.

This is false, not only because we cannot always successfully draw the line between the two, but also, above all, because in certain cases it is particularly necessary to report the intentional willful harming of others. More important than the distinction between different *kinds* of violence is the difference between *methods* of depicting them. Thus the decisive factors are the intentions of the producers, the means they use, and the effects—intentional or unintentional—that they produce.

The media can portray willful violence in such a way as to make an effective protest against physical and psychic harm to human beings. Or they can picture accidents or catastrophes in a way that will satisfy the viewers' hunger for sensations without awakening their pity for the victims. If one were to use the categories of intentional and unintentional violence, for instance, how should one evaluate films showing suicides? "The leap of a man from a thirty-foot-high bridge and his impact on the road beneath was shown—as though it were a sports event—once at regular speed, and once in slow motion."

Today's knowledge of suicides does not permit ranking them among intentional acts of violence, so one should probably assign this scene to the more harmless category. Yet the means used to film it had the opposite effect of titillating the viewers. The producers deemed it permissible to make a fatally unhappy person an instrument of entertainment. The objection to this is obviously an ethical one.

THE ROLE OF ETHICS

Ethics are in a weak position when faced with the powers that shape the development of the media. We should have no illusions on this point. As early as 1980, Maximilian Gottschlich already gave a good explanation for this weakness in relation to journalism. I will illustrate these reasons from my own perspective.

First, there is no question that journalism not only must consider but also is committed to, to some extent, a pluralism in ethical orientation. What would a normative orientation for journalistic behavior look like, if journalism itself should present the variety of such normative orientations in a fair and impartial way? Why should the perspective of Christian ethics have more authority than that of Islamic or Marxist or nihilistic ethics, or even no ethic at all?

Second, ethical arguments bounce off the professional reality without effect. Just as the only thing that counts in a market economy is whatever strengthens competition, so does the media count on increased circulation, high ratings, and high returns from advertising. To bring up ethical arguments in this reality would only falsely idealize professional reality.

Third, what is even worse is that a normative ethic of journalism would only serve to cover up the actual circumstances of this dependency and to hide the true economically determined pressures with a pious robe.

Fourth, even if a journalistic ethic existed, it would not be enforceable, since it does not have any sanctioning authority. The censure of peer organizations can be comfortably ignored. When one person sticks to an ethical standard and refuses to show certain pictures, the others laugh up their sleeves.

Even though an ethic is in a position of weakness when confronting the power of the media, thoughtful people cannot reject it, for human life does not consist of just the one magnetic pole of self-assertion in a fight and holding one's own in competition. Human life is also attracted to the other pole: respect for another person and solidarity with the neighbor. Not even in the media can success be separated from responsibility for the consequences.

Max Weber is the source for the problematic, mostly misquoted, differentiation—impossible to wipe out of any discussion of ethics—between the ethic of principle and the ethic of responsibility. The ethicist of principle, speaking religiously, says, "The Christian does a good deed and credits God with the success." The ethicist of responsibility knows "that one must be accountable for the foreseeable consequences of one's actions."[9]

Even I must return to Weber's differentiation, because the opinion is spreading within the media that "a bit of irresponsibility" is part of doing effective work in the media. The argument goes that journalists are not responsible to make sure the city, state, and nation are governed successfully. Neither the government's correct nor its wrong decisions should be blamed on journalists. They are not responsible for the consequences resulting from the publication of a fact. And what is valid for news should also be valid for entertainment programs. It is said that the use viewers make of the media's offerings is not the responsibility of the media. They are not responsible for the aggressiveness that is aroused or increased by their presentations of violence. They do not have to feel responsible for the brutalization that can result from their intrusion into human privacy.

RESPONSIBILITY FOR ONE'S OWN ACTIONS

Producers do bear a responsibility for their own actions, if not for the actions on which they report. They are responsible for the consequences released by their investigations as well as by the events they picture. The people who present violence for entertainment and make intimacy an instrument of it must be held responsible for their actions. They must be accountable for the integrity of people they have turned into instruments of entertainment, both the living and the dead.

I share the view of Klaus Bresser, who wrote, "Besides speed, currency, and accuracy as to facts, we must pose a further demand on our work: consideration for the victims, sympathy for the sufferers. That is why we will take the liberty to reject the use of certain pictures, even when we know there is a market for them." [10]

PRINCIPLES FOR A UNIVERSALIST ETHIC

I never liked talk of the media as the "Fourth Estate," for journalism makes use of no autonomous power. It does not ally itself with the three powers that do exercise the authority of the state. Yet one statement concerning the power of the state should at least be applicable to journalism as well: "the dignity of human beings is inalienable." To respect and protect such dignity is precisely the responsibility not just of the government but of journalism as well. Journalism has been provided with fundamentally guaranteed civil rights so as to use the standard of human dignity to check on and criticize the exercise of governmental power. But its critique is credible only when it applies the criteria it uses on others on itself as well.

Despite all our pluralism and ethical relativism, we must— even with regard to journalism—seek those ethical criteria that all those to whom they are applicable can accept with due deliberation and without force. We must seek that "issue common to all humanity" that can be justifiably considered universal.

The fact that I respect the dignity of the other just as much as I depend upon respect from others for my own dignity is an elementary aspect of a universalist ethic. I always use this ethic as soon as I start communicating on the basis of equality with another human being. In every exchange with an equal I am forced to grant the other the freedom I myself have. Consequently, I can never view others as merely means; I must acknowledge them as ends in themselves—that is precisely where the dignity of persons is found.

For a long time, in so far as we acknowledged this dignity at all, we saw it as a prerogative of the human species, the crown of creation. Only now does it dawn on us that our fellow creatures possess a dignity that should not be simply delivered up to the selfish use and unfettered exploitation of other human beings. Thus the core of a universalist ethic is not just respect for human dignity but respect for all living things.

This respect should also constitute the core of media ethics. Only within that framework is competition a legitimate instrument of control. If competition violates that framework, it loses its legitimacy. Just because there is a market for treating living things with contempt is not a justification for sharing this contempt or even profiting from it.

I do not want to suggest that today's producers do not know the universalist principles to which I have just referred. Indeed, I think that they are familiar with these ethical criteria. Nor do I know of a prescription to resolve the tension they have to maintain these ethical criteria and also to make their daily decisions.

I only know one guideline that can give our conscience a better hearing when making decisions: slowness. I therefore describe the dilemma in which journalists find themselves daily as the conflict between the slowness of conscience and the quickness of actual events. When competition for ratings and shares of the leisure market is the all-decisive criterion, quickness all too often wins over slowness. To put it differently: topicality wins over conscience.

TELEVISION AND THE BAN ON IMAGES

Television culture, when it becomes pervasive, violates the spirit of the Hebrew Bible's "ban on images." For the Israelites, the ban on making images of God was the precondition for freedom. The freedom of God and human beings depended on obedience to the command, "You shall not make for yourself an idol, whether in the form of anything that is in heaven above or that is on the earth beneath, or that is in the water under the earth. You shall not bow down to them or worship them" (Exod. 20:4–5).

All who lock God into an image transgress against divine freedom and worship an idol they have made for themselves. But they also gamble away their own freedom, because this freedom is based on our being created in God's image and therefore not tied to any images others make of us: "You shall not make for yourself an idol."

Max Frisch noted that the possibility of love depends on maintaining the ban on images.[11] Only when we do not tie others to the images we have made of them do we honor their freedom and thus leave room for love. Christians confess a God who refuses to be tied to any image made by human beings, and instead freely is tied to the image of a human being. God's own freedom is honored only where the dignity of human beings is acknowledged. Whoever violates or defames the dignity of a human being denies God.

A total, unlimited television culture not only allows the blurring of fact and fiction, it also replaces the freedom of humans with images of them. What is important in this culture is not who I am but who others think I am. The great alternative today is not, as Erich Fromm said, "to have or to be," but rather "to show or to be."

Christian ethics will have to defend the precedence of being over showing, even when the market for it is limited, for this defense serves the possibility of love and solidarity, and therefore human freedom. Those who orient themselves to this bias are still hoping for media which do not exploit the vulnerability of people but instead protect people. It is this function of protection that forms the decisive boundary against all use of violence and intimidation for the sake of entertainment.

CHAPTER TWO

Taking Liberties with Human Dignity

The Example of Sports

B en Johnson, the Canadian athlete of Jamaican extraction, was a universally celebrated idol. In 1987, he set a new world record time of 9.83 seconds for the 100-meter race at the World Competition in Rome. One year later, at the summer Olympic Games in Seoul, his gold medal was snatched from him after testing revealed steroid use. He had achieved his excellence in sports by using illegal drugs and doing violence to his own body. He not only cheated his competitors, he cheated the world public.

Johnson fell as far as he had previously risen. His case made waves; steroid use became the topic of the day. One scandal after another was exposed, yet disciplinary actions lagged far behind strong language.

With the exception of drug use, nothing threatens the integrity of sports as much as its increasing violence. "Fair play," the traditional standard of sports, is no longer its hallmark. A fair contest requires, above all, obeying the rules of the game and taking care not to injure the opponent. This has been turned upside down in many kinds of athletic activity. It is no comfort to know that these scandals apply only to a small number of sports. It is still scandalous.

North Americans may think of football or hockey, but Europeans like myself think of soccer. Calculated violation of the rules is a part of training goals, and anyone not prepared to commit a foul no longer has any business on the soccer field. Saturday after Saturday millions of viewers watch as players attack their opponents rather than the ball. The sport is surrounded by scandals, usually involving great sums of money.

Violence on the soccer field is equalled by violence in the stands. Fans of competing teams must be separated by high fences. One of the most important police duties after a game is to make sure the rampaging hooligans are escorted out of town before getting a chance to do much damage.

Countless people in Europe and America regularly take part in some athletic activity—usually far removed from manipulation and violence. Many types of athletics remain untouched by the well-known scandals in football, baseball, soccer and track and field. They are not in the spotlight, and are of no interest to TV ratings. It would nevertheless be näive to point to the wide range of sports relatively untouched by scandal in order to dismiss the danger to athletics as unimportant. Athletics in general suffer from a credibility crisis.

Sports, which should serve human growth and health, have become a threat to the dignity of human beings. The dignity of human beings is inalienable, we have said, but sports demonstrate that this dignity can be encroached upon. Human dignity must be willed, indeed must be fought for, but it is no longer self-evident that sports obey any of these ethical principles.

Sports have no particular ethic of their own. The decisive ethical criteria used by human beings in the past and used now never were and are not now limited to sports. Most of these criteria were not even set to apply solely to sports. Anyone who is aware of this is well advised not to call for an ethic peculiar to sports, but instead to look for general ethical principles that also apply to sports. Of course these principles must apply to the particular challenges now facing sports as well. To put it another way: they must apply to the challenges with which ethics now confronts sports.

THE MEANING OF SPORT

But what is sport really? Many people participate in athletics, but what they really do is subject to argument. I shall deal here with two specific themes: the significance of sports and the leading principles of sports.

The first topic is the concept and significance of sports. Dietrich Kurz, in summarizing an extensive discussion, has pointed out that there is no longer a short, handy formula available to define sport. We can best understand what sport is when we seek the meaning people give to it, and what they look for in sports. Consequently, the very question of the definition of sport already contains an ethical dimension, since it can only be understood on the basis of the intentions people have in connection with it. Sports do not exist independently of the intentions with which people participate in them. In fact, Kurz has distinguished six such intentions:

(1) People seek particular experiences of the body in athletic activities: physical equilibrium, physical challenge—as comprehensive as possible—and the sense of well-being that results. They also expect positive results to affect their physical fitness, their health, and their shape.

(2) People seek the stimulation, the sensations, and the joy that can be linked to the act of movement itself. They open themselves through the athletic movements to particular kinds of experience—not excluding experiences in and over nature.

(3) People seek to shape a message about themselves: they want to express something in their movements. They want to have their movements appear expert, artistic, impressive, beautiful, and aesthetic.

(4) People seek a field of activity in which they can expect to demand something of themselves, measure improvement, compare themselves to others, recognize their possibilities and limitations, and experience the respect of others and a sense of their own worth.

(5) People seek an open-ended situation that provides tension but does not necessarily endanger them. They seek experiences of risk and adventure, the excitement of the unknown, and the sense of relief that results afterwards.

(6) People seek togetherness with others, the particular and often freer kind of conversation, the experience of closeness, conviviality, and community.[1]

This comprehensible description can lead us to an understanding of athletics as a whole. It spotlights the significant dimensions in such a way that we can still recognize the unity of recreational sport, competitive sport, and spectator sport. I combine all of these into an image first used to describe human work: work can best be understood in terms of a triangle, its three points being the natural, the personal, and the social dimensions of life. The same image applies to athletics.

Sports have a *natural* dimension, a way of acting in which people make use of the natural conditions of their own lives and of their own physical existence. As a rule, it takes the form of exercise in space and time, combining human nature with the natural environment. This physical exercise has an important criterion and an important goal in matters of both health and physical well-being.

Sports have a *personal* dimension that is useful in developing personal worth. Sports are an expression of human creativity and organizing ability. Human beings confront their own unity of body, soul, and intellect in athletic activity.

Sports have a *social* dimension, for human beings encounter each other in sports. They realize that they are dependent on each other and enrich each other; that they challenge each other and can compete against each other.

The ambivalence of sports has thus already been characterized in the above description. Athletics, both individual physical exercise and competitive sports, can serve the unfolding of human worth. But sports can also imperil this worth, and this too occurs in all aspects of athletics, not just in highly competitive sports. Consequently, responsible behavior in sports has the duty to suppress the dangerous moments and help bring out the unfolding of the life-enhancing moments.

This kind of responsible behavior finds itself in increasing difficulties today. The balance between the three dimensions of sports is teetering, because the urge to achieve personal enhancement and self-realization often wins out over the social dimension. The desire to confront one's own nature and increase one's own strength topples over into damaging one's own body—and often the whole person.

On the whole, the threatening tendencies in sports are linked in one way or another to the intensification of violence in sports and of violence caused by sports. Included in these threats to sports are increased violence in boxing matches—the sport featured as the sport of violence—the drug use of athletes, other forms of manipulating achievement, violence among fans, and the linkage of sports to nationalistic or other types of fanaticism.

A commitment to the primacy of nonviolence over all types of violence, and therefore to the elimination of violence as such, is of practical importance at this point. No longer can one passively accept any prognoses regarding sports that count on further intensification of hidden aggressiveness and overt brutality, or on an increase in the health-threatening manipulation of achievement. On the contrary, more outspokenness and more definite action are required.

PRINCIPLES OF SPORTS

Responsible behavior in sports is becoming simultaneously more difficult and more urgently needed. However, we do not start from scratch. Instead, we start with experiences, which leads me to the second theme. Ommo Grupe has proposed six principles characterizing the expanded self-understanding of athletics. I quote them here:

> *First* is the appeal to the ideal and universally useful character of sports. Sports should consider itself to be social and pedagogical;

it should be open to as many people as possible; and its funda-
mentals should include honorary officials, its own organization,
and its own achievements. Consequently it should not concern
itself with money or profit.

Second is the demand that athletic activity should be voluntary and without compulsion. Its accompanying presupposition
is that athletic activity can unfold its particular advantages only
when this is the case.

Third is the emphasis on the significance of sports for the
health and well-being of people in a world characterized by a
growing lack of movement and impoverishment of movement.

Fourth is the dependence on its social significance based on
fairness and solidarity in a society which especially needs common interests.

Fifth is its trust in its educational effect especially on children
and young people.

Sixth is the bond between its ideas and praxis and its understanding of human beings, which stresses their worth and inviolability and takes seriously their need for play, movement, health,
and community, as well as their need for achievement and competition.[2]

The measured self-understanding of sports has been plausi-
bly formulated in these six principles. My summary makes use
of the triangle image again, stating that the sports triangle rests
on a foundation composed of the following six building blocks
(I have ranked them a little differently from Grupe): openness,
voluntariness, health, fairness, education, community. These
six building blocks are held together by respect for the dignity
and inviolability of human beings.

As comprehensible as these principles are, it is necessary to
add that this self-understanding is today anything but obvious.
Rather, it is undermined and threatened with erosion. That
is why we must turn to the changes to which athletics are
exposed.

EFFECTS OF SOCIAL CHANGE

The social changes occurring in the 1980s and their meaning
for sports have been described often. Nevertheless, the extent

and drama of these changes are perhaps still being underesti- mated. I cannot, of course, describe all these changes in detail, so I shall confine myself to three factors.

(1) The 1980s will be remembered as having initiated a mighty push toward the individualization of lifestyles. People no longer live according to a standardized design shaped by family or personal conviction. Instead, they shape their lives more in the fashion of a patchwork quilt, which is why one speaks of "patchwork identity." Many people are no longer con- cerned with the primary effect of certain actions on the com- munity. Instead, they are guided by personal benefits or by an action's meaning for their own self-realization. The American sociologist Robert N. Bellah and other American authors have called the dominant attitude of those now of the younger gen- eration "utilitarian individualism" and "expressive individu- alism." [3]

This shift has had a direct effect on the conduct of sports. Jogging or solitary walking denote the types of athletic activity characteristic of the decade. Individual body work in health clubs serves expressive individualism. Team sports are losing importance. Individualization of lifestyles is reflected in all areas of sports—although, paradoxically, the behavior consid- ered individual is copied profusely. One need only observe the many individualists who jog over a popular running track at the very same time and often in the very same outfits as the other joggers.

(2) The "public person" has undergone a transformation as well. "Public persons" are those who bear a particular impor- tance for the normative self-understanding of a society. In tradi- tional, as well as more modern, societies, these were officials of some kind, such as princes or bishops, captains of industry or presidents, party leaders or cabinet ministers, pastors or teach- ers. They were considered models of behavior, and if they failed to live up to expectations, disappointment was relatively great. These officials were considered standard-bearers—if for no

other reason, because due to their office they bore the responsibility for the general welfare—for that which unites a society and thus binds its members to it.

But a subjectivization of personhood accompanies individualization of lifestyles. We no longer accept officials telling us what is good for our society, nor do we believe that their behavior is guided by what is good for society. Many people reject the very concept of society's good as socially romantic. As a result, officials suffer a tremendous loss of credibility and popularity. "Political irritation" is a latent problem in our society that, when exacerbating errors are added, can quickly become overt. A certain "church irritation" is spreading as well: the loss of authority on the part of church officials is beginning to have an effect.

Meanwhile, other "public persons" are taking the place of these former standard-bearers. Public attention is drawn particularly to those who express most extremely and forcefully the individuality of human beings. These people are, for the most part, star athletes and pop musicians. The former demonstrate augmented individuality through their bodies' outstanding achievements; the latter do so through the musical portrayal of their emotionalism. Steffi Graf in tennis or Michael Jordan in basketball on the one hand, and singers Michael Jackson or Madonna on the other, have been turned into public persons in whom the public's yearning for personhood and individuality is crystallized.

Today the stars of entertainment and sports are the most important public persons, supplanting bishops, politicians, and writers. And yet there is a shift occurring in sports itself, which could perhaps be reduced to the formula "from Jesse Owens to Carl Lewis," meaning from an approachable model to an unequaled individual. The mass media often surround today's stars with a quasi-religious aura. Their public appearances sometimes become ecstatic cultural events, with all the dangers to life and limb that can result from displays of ecstasy.

The athletes' role as "public persons" in the way I have described it, carries tremendous consequences for the field of sports (my Heidelberg colleague Michael Welker brought it to my attention[4]), for it separates athletics in general from competitive sports even more than used to be the case. What leads to the rift between the spectator sports broadcast by the media and the athletic pursuits of individual persons is not so much the fact that achievements in sports are rising to dizzying heights, but rather the fact that star athletes appear as cultic symbols of their own yearning for individuality.

(3) Competitive sports have been deeply interwoven with politics in the past few decades, not only as a means of national self-expression but also as an instrument in the struggle between political systems. The build-up of sports on both sides, the compensatory importance in the East of victories in sport in relation to its economic inferiority, or the direct use of politics in sports by the U.S.A., West Germany, and several other nations in boycotting the Moscow Olympic Games of 1980 clearly illustrate my point.

The East-West conflict collapsed in 1989. This collapse brought about the most extensive political regroupings and inversions seen on this planet since the end of World War II. Sports, like all other areas of life, is being drawn into the resulting changes.

One particular consequence of this change is that public funds are being redistributed, and the struggle for these funds is getting more intense. Anyone engaged in public activity could lend his/her name every day to some important project, the continuation of which in its present form has been endangered by government cutbacks: today in opposition to cutbacks in labor assistance; tomorrow in support of full funding for music schools; the next day in support of sports.

I have called another developmental trend resulting from the changes of these years "from world politics to world economics." By this I mean that until the 1980s, the global constellation—even insofar as it was shaped economically—was thought of in categories of conflict between political systems, but now it is seen primarily from the perspective of worldwide economic competition. Many aspects of life are being placed in the service of this competition more extensively than heretofore.

This applies to competitive sports in a very special way. True, the commercialization of competitive sports is not a new phenomenon. But now it is increasing, with no known countervailing force in sight. Economic interests, directed in large measure by economic centers or powers, determine the sites for the Olympic games—Seoul in 1988, Barcelona 1992, Atlanta 1996—as investigative reports have demonstrated.

The professional manner with which not just leagues but also international sports federations conduct their affairs as profitable business undertakings arouses the understandable greed of the athletes. In turn, athletes make their performing at sports festivals and international competitions dependent on ever-increasing financial compensation. This was most blatantly demonstrated in the U.S. baseball strike of 1994–95.

The Olympics movement is a kind of showcase for sports as a whole so it is not unfair to view its development as an example of athletics as a whole as well. The Olympic games reveal a coherent pattern that can be stated as "this part of sports is essentially shaped by the media and by marketing interests." Their method of arriving at decisions has at times a mafia-like tinge.

The emphasis on material interests, which predominates among the producers and functionaries is, logically, carried over to the athletes. The result is a kind of competition in which victory, not achievement, is the decisive factor.

The indifference to achievement and the one-sided interest in success have far-reaching consequences. Whoever comes in second or third in no-matter-how-great a race is asked only to explain the loss. The achievement counts for nothing. Since success is decisive, for better or worse, there is a built-in tendency in the system to manipulate that achievement. Consequently, steroid use, in a sport shaped by the world market, does not violate but rather conforms to the system.

Steroid use, however, is an act of aggression not only against the human body but also against truth, for it no longer permits a realistic judgment of an athlete's ability, and it tempts athletes to cover up by all available means the manipulation of their own bodies. The new world records we have witnessed are logically tied to a development in which international competitions are no longer even considered to be supporting national pride but are instead merely the instruments of world market competition. Anyone shocked by steroid use must not turn a blind eye to its context.

ETHIC OF DIGNITY OR ETHIC OF INTERESTS

The result of all this is that human dignity is vulnerable to encroachment. Athletics have become a front on which the conflict between two fundamentally distinct orientations is taking place.

The first I call the "ethic of dignity." It is nourished by the religious insight that human beings are created in the image of God. Humans do not have control of themselves, but instead have received their value as a gift. This value is false precisely when humans insist on being in control of their own lives, when they high-handedly want to determine the meaning of their own lives, when—according to the profound insight of the Jewish and Christian faith—they want to be like God. At this point people transgress against God, against their fellow creatures, and against themselves. They alienate themselves, in guilt and sin, from their life's destiny. Christian faith trusts that God is loyal even to these alienated humans, that God opens new beginnings to them, grants them strength, offers them reconciliation, and calls them into the service of reconciliation.

Philosophy adopted this concept in secular form when it referred to the dignity of humans and put this dignity into the categorical imperative never to see others or themselves as merely means but always as ends in themselves as well.

An ethic of dignity takes care never to use other people or oneself merely as instruments to obtain a goal but always to respect others and oneself as subjects. Sports is one of the most intensive forms in which humans use themselves as means to an end and as instruments to a goal. It is therefore that much more necessary to keep to the parameters set by the dignity of human beings: never must the subject human being be sacrificed to the goal of sports. The ethic of dignity encompasses consideration for both individual and collective interests. It does not intend to reject interests but desires instead to set the parameters within which they are permitted to operate.

These parameters are not sufficiently considered in the ethical position I have called the "ethic of interests," which is propounded by the Australian writer Peter Singer, for example, and by German authors like Norbert Hoerster or Dieter Birnbacker. They have no use for the thought of human dignity, because they argue that this thought is perceivable only against the religious background of belief that humans exist in God's image. These authors insist that such a religious assertion cannot be made plausible to a pluralistic and therefore religiously neutral society, and so it is no longer permissible to advance this view in questions of public moral relevance either. Moreover, these philosophers are convinced that modern constitutions, such as Article I of the Bonn Constitution, do not alter this position in any way.

In an ethic of interests, moral questions are decided on the basis of the preferences of the persons involved. Thus, if an athlete prefers to achieve athletic success for himself, and to be well compensated for it, nothing can be said against it. Above all, no superior standard exists against which this preference could be measured. Nor can there be any objection when athletes prefer to place less value on their own body's integrity. What must be avoided in that case is the stress when competing that can result from the manipulation of their own bodies, although this occurs only when the use of drugs is taboo and covert. If drug use is practiced openly, then everyone has the option of using drugs, and the decision to do so depends solely on one's preference. If one carried this ethic of interests to its conclusion, then consistency would lie in permission to use drugs rather than in strict prohibition.

Comparable positions utilizing the standard of preferences or ethic of interest have been publicly advanced on the issues of abortion, biological and genetic manipulation of persons, killing of severely handicapped newborn infants, and euthanasia. The gravity of the ethical conflicts at issue is regularly rendered innocuous in these discussions, and the same applies in sports in the case of drug-using athletes, the ethical and legal deregulation of which is the result of the ethic of interests.

No compromise is possible between these two basic orientations, and a decision is unavoidable. I emphasize again: the exclusion of interests and preferences from ethical considerations is not the issue. On the contrary, it is necessary to determine the meaning of both as accurately as possible. It is legitimate to pursue one's interests and preferences. But that legitimacy is valid only as long as one's own dignity as well as the dignity of others is protected. Furthermore, it is valid only when the value of nonhuman nature is respected as well. Interests and preferences must not be lived out at the expense of human dignity. Nor may they result in humans assuming the right to exploit and destroy nature because they are the "masters and possessors of nature," to quote René Descartes. Interests and preferences must not be allowed to rule our thinking and behavior without restrictions, for they are restricted by the equal value of all humans and by respect for the value of nature.

If the humanity of sports, a most deeply human activity, is to be preserved, the double restriction must be observed. The manipulation of hormones and using drugs to influence achievement are incompatible with the equal value of human beings.

THE OLYMPIC MODEL OR THE JESUS MODEL

The fundamental conflict presently especially noticeable in sports, though in no way limited to sports, can be described in another way. On the one hand, one aspect of the concept of human dignity is that all humans should be supported in their dignity and developmental possibilities, even—indeed, particularly—when their physical abilities are impaired and their choice of lifestyles is restricted. Modern competitive society, on the other hand, measures the worth of human beings primarily and exclusively according to their achievements. One of the dangers in an achievement-oriented society is that this support for the dignity of all is suppressed. This society easily ignores the insight that the humaneness of a lifestyle is not shown by the way it values achievements but is instead shown by the way it makes room for those incapable or limited in ability, and treats them with respect. Only "people ready for the Olympics" are suitable for modern methods of production, according to a well-informed contemporary.

It has been demonstrated that whoever intends to provide employment to persons with physical disabilities—or even more, to persons with psychological or mental disabilities—must provide a sheltered space where the rules of the market economy are suspended. Industrial competitive society itself does not provide that space.

The attitude toward life represented by a competitive society is that the dignity and right to life of a human being are tied to a minimum measure of autonomy, orientation to the future, and ability to perform. The dignity of those who do not have control over their own lives, who do not orient themselves to the future, or who are not able to support themselves, is thus easily overlooked. That is why it is quite logical that it is precisely in this kind of society that notions of "lives not worth living" surface and find a hearing. The meaning of human life, according to the predominant image, is revealed in health, beauty, ability to perform, and strength. Illness, impairment, and death are out of bounds, pushed to the outer edge, and considered heretical under some circumstances.

Ulrich Bach, a theologian who has been confined to a wheelchair for decades, has described this dichotomy in society with the caustic and mordant term "social racism." I call the image of humanity supporting it the "Olympic model." To speak of an "Olympic" model does not mean that I compare the ancient or the modern Olympic games with this model in every detail. Rather, I want to characterize a particular, basically typical, attitude of society, which is clearly connected with Olympic sports.

This Olympic model orients itself towards the flawless, youthful, achieving victor. It is a basically male model and has a particularly good chance of succeeding in a society dominated to a large extent by male values and interests. It stamps the reality of the sport in large measure, as is clearly demonstrated by separating the Olympic Games for the able-bodied athletes from the Special Olympic Games for physically and mentally challenged persons.

Christian faith confronts this model with another image of mankind, which I call the "Jesus model." Israel's image of humans, which Jesus adopted, expanded, and imparted to others through the conduct of his life, takes seriously the limitation and vulnerability of other humans. This image encourages us to accept the mortality of our own life and that of strangers. It does not glorify illness—how could one then explain the healings by Jesus?—but it does not degrade the sick, the physically and mentally challenged, and the aged to second-class humans. It stresses that everybody—irrespective of age, gender, citizenship, religion, achievement or merit—is due the same dignity, precisely in the face of our human vulnerability and mortality.

The Jesus model draws us into a continuous change of perspective. True, most Christians, too, pay more attention to a tennis pro of great achievement than to a person with muscular dystrophy who laboriously seeks a way to gain independence in a sheltered workshop. Yet the Jesus model enables us to at least interrupt our interest in the tennis pro and pay attention to the one who has so much more difficulty and, measured by his or her capability, also achieves so much more.

Everyone is of equal worth. That also means that especially those who have great difficulty in being autonomous people are dependent on signs of our appreciation. We know that no one can be independent without having received at least a minimum of appreciation.

If I call this the Jesus model, in contradistinction to the Olympic one, I do not mean to say that Christians can claim exclusive ownership of it. Its method of thinking is deeply anchored in the history of Israel, and it has sometimes been more clearly represented by modern secular convictions of the equal worth of all humans and by secular solidarity with the helpless than by the decisions and behavior of the large Christian churches. None of these are excluded from my description of the Jesus model. But it should be remembered clearly who gave decisive shape to this model of humanity for the Christian faith and for others as well.

ACHIEVEMENT AND SUCCESS

We can gain access to human achievement only when we recognize that human beings have limitations, when we understand that mortality and vulnerability are essential attributes of human beings. We can appreciate a person's achievement only when we compare it to that person's capability. We appreciate our own achievements only when we become aware of our own limitations in achieving them. To achieve something means to do something well. Athletic competition is an indicator to see whether, when measured against our own possibilities and the possibilities of others in comparable situations, we did something well—whether we dealt creatively and productively with our own limitations.

In such a view of achievement, the athletic achievements of the handicapped can be honored just as much as those of the physically unimpaired. Viewed this way, it is possible to let children pursue athletic activities within their own framework of abilities without driving them prematurely and with negative results into intense achievement. The absorption in children's high achievement really occurs when the decisive factor is not achievement but success.

Success is not concerned with the question of whether one did well when compared to one's ability, but rather whether one did better than others. If one was not the best, the only question is "Why?"—the famous question reporters ask those who come in second. When this question is posed it is the Olympic model that wins out, and this model is incompatible with the Christian image of humanity.

Consequently, sports maintain their humanity only when they refuse to be absorbed by the thought of competition, by the Olympic model, and by the reality of the world market economy, but instead regain a certain distance from those factors. Undoubtedly, there are some areas in athletics that are not victims of this absorption, or at least can maintain their distance. The implementation of these considerations can protect these areas, including some competitive sports, and possibly expand them. The commercialization of world-class competitive sports cannot be revoked. But clear boundaries should be set to that sphere in order to prevent its spread to other athletic activities.

In commercialized sports it is probably impossible to defend the dignity of humans by ethical means. Only legal measures will work. Steroid use will not be prevented by voluntary self-discipline but only by enforcing the law. The intentional and crudely overlooked injuring of opposition players must also be much more rigorously prosecuted than heretofore. In any case, sports should not produce the violence so eagerly broadcast by the media.

SPORTS AND VALUE OF NATURE

Sports, according to the reflections I have presented so far, must consider two boundary lines: the dignity of human beings, and the preservation of nature. I do not intend to go into the latter as deeply as I did the former, but instead will introduce the following points.

Over time, sport and environmental protection have been thought of as competing goals. On the one hand is the interest in constructing sports stadiums, on the other is the interest in preserving biotopes. On the one hand is the noise emanating from athletic events, on the other is the desire for silence amid natural beauty. I do not mean to belittle these conflicts, for they have arisen from these opposite goals. I just want to point out that sport will only lose its ethical defensiveness when, much more clearly than at present, it gains a more positive attitude to the preservation of the natural environment.

When the discussion first began in Germany on whether the preservation of natural environments should be included in our constitution as a national goal, the first reaction from the ranks of athletes was that in that case one should make the support of sports a national goal too. I consider this a false reaction, and the German Athletic League's Council for Constitutional Issues also counseled against it, with good reason.

It would be wiser and more effective if sports would, for its own sake, take a clear stand in support of such a national goal to "preserve the natural life forms," and if it would also make plain that the athletic movement is concerned with not merely representing the league's interests, but also with contributing to the totality of human life. This totality is endangered if we do not succeed in changing our relationship to nature, on which our lives depend.

To acknowledge the preservation of nature as a frontier of human activity also has consequences for sports. If this acknowledgment is taken seriously, then the slogan "sport for everyone" cannot be taken to mean unlimited expansion and nature-exploiting types of sport. It would not then be sensible, for example, to cling too stubbornly to erecting a sport facility in a specific place, even though there are unanimous ecological objections to the site and alternative solutions have been offered (but this kind of stubbornness still exists). Sports should be in the forefront of the ecological reorganization that is inevitable in industrial society instead of being a reluctant laggard.

INDIVIDUALITY AND SOCIABILITY

I have distinguished three dimensions of sports: the natural, the personal, and the social. The push toward individualization during the 1980s moved the personal dimension into the foreground, and the significance of athletics for the development, presentation, and realization of individual persons took center stage. As we saw, this endangered the natural dimension, for self-improvement veered into self-endangerment and, in extreme cases, into self-destruction. That is why conscious, planned, and decisive countermeasures must be undertaken. A change in orientation does not happen by itself. But it can always succeed when it is clearly intended and carried though decisively, even against opposition. In this connection, the discussion on drug use acquires a more than symbolic significance.

But the social dimension of sport is also threatened, as many phenomena indicate, such as the decrease in team sports, the increased violence in competitive sports and among sports fans, the association of sports with nationalism, and the burgeoning commercialization and big business dimensions of sports.

True, one cannot force people to experience community; one cannot command them to be sociable; solidarity cannot be enforced. Yet one cannot watch with indifference when the relationship between individuality and sociability gets out of balance in a whole society.

The consequences of this imbalance can be seen in many areas today. In Germany, the crudest example is the violence against strangers and the applause or indifference that have accompanied this violence for a long time. Only now, following the terrible intensification of hostility toward aliens and the murderous violence does a shudder go through the German public.

This shudder also went through sports. The first explanations regarding the enmity of foreigners, made by sports leaders in September 1992, did not yet resonate very much in public. But perhaps greater weight should be put on an attitude that one commentator described:

> It should be self-evident that all sports leagues strenuously oppose all forms of xenophobia and hostility against foreigners, and that they energetically attack all racial discrimination in our country. The leagues are challenged not only to integrate and to care for aliens in everyday sports activities, but also to do everything they can to oppose every kind of political radicalism and persecution of foreigners, and in this way influence public opinion. It is possible that this requires a certain amount of civil courage.[5]

This kind of civil courage is surely promoted when athletic leagues like the German Handball League make the slogan "Hate for foreigners—not with us!" their centerpiece. Such actions turn the climate from social coldness to concern for fellow humans, from indifference and turning away to civil courage, from exclusion of the stranger to equality in community, from uninhibited individualism to a new balance between self-realization and solidarity.

Any politics of sports that wants to oppose sports-specific violence effectively must set different priorities than the ones that presently prevail. It must set greater importance on the dignity of humans than on success, more importance on being at home in a supportive community than on success as an individual, more importance on looking for credible models than on spotlighting stars.

Such a politics would consider it more important to differentiate between what people can do and what they can be responsible for doing than to increase what can be done, more important to have consideration for the weak than to triumph over them, more important to work for peace in one world than to have national success. It would reject without compromise the kind of success that can only be obtained by manipulating one's own body and by violent aggression against one's opponent.

CHAPTER THREE

The Society of the Majority and the Minorities

Conditions of Living Together

riday, November 27, 1992: In Hamburg, 10,000 people are attending a memorial service for Bahide Arslan, Yelzin Arslan, and Asye Yilmaz, three Turkish women murdered out of ethnic hatred, an incident noted internationally.

More than 400 miles away, in Kork, a celebration is being held to commemorate the centenary of the Epilepsy Center, a diaconal institution of the Lutheran Church. But the celebration is overshadowed by growing concern that the acts of aggression directed against foreigners today could also strike other minorities. Even when only a few groups of people decide to resort to the use of violence and ruthless criminality, they do so in a favorable climate. This sort of social coldness has given rise to a sense of fear and danger that forces people toward practical solidarity. Is it already too late to repulse these early acts?

Saturday, November 28: All the democratic forces—mainstream political parties, churches, and special interest groups—have called for a gathering today in Heidelberg and in many other cities to demonstrate against the hostility and violence practiced against foreigners. An estimated 7,000 to 8,000 people participate, patiently listening to the speeches in spite of the rain.

When one person declares that finally the German public has been given a shock, it sounds convincing, but in many places the shock is slow to make itself felt. The rector of the university at Heidelberg reminds me that it is not the style of their teaching body to take to the streets. I ask myself whether it could possibly be the style of a university to participate in the defense of human rights.

Nor is shrillness lacking. Catcalls greet the speaker from the Christian Democrat party, as well as cries of "Hypocrite!" Some of the speakers exaggerate, not just for oratorical reasons. One speaker declares, "Everything foreign is an enrichment to us," a lovely generality. My wife whispers to me, "That isn't true." The next day I would understand her objection better.

Sunday, November 29: My wife and I visit three foreign families in the afternoon. She has long been active in a group that assists refugees, and, as an elementary school teacher, she has contact with foreign families.

The first visit is to a Gypsy family from Rumania. Their son has been attending third grade for the past three months. All efforts to get the parents to talk to their child's teacher have failed so far. My wife has learned in the meantime that she cannot comfort herself by pointing out the Gypsy cultural particularity. She must persevere and awaken the parents' understanding of the rule stating that parents take an interest in their children's schooling, and she now tries to explain in plain, simple words.

The second visit is to an Albanian extended family. An attempt had been made to find employment for the woman. She was to iron seven shirts a week for a German white collar worker, but the attempt failed, because only six shirts were returned. A job as cleaning woman also failed: on the first day she did not show up for work because her father-in-law came to visit; the second time it was because her child was ill. Her husband rejected a job at a supermarket, because he would have had to interview for the position, and he found that distasteful.

My wife tries to explain to them the reaction of their prospective employers. We hope that the combined efforts of the extended family have overcome the language barrier. Will it work next time? For the moment, three chances for employment have been lost.

Our last visit is to a family from the Kosovo. There are six daughters in the family, the oldest of whom is eight years old. The father has not yet abandoned his desire for a son. The two oldest girls attend my wife's class in their first year of school. They were once invited to the home of some German children. After the visit, it was discovered that a hair ribbon, a chain with a pacifier, and five marks were missing. Would we succeed in making them understand what the consequences would be if such incidents reoccurred—if they ever did get invited into a German home again? The ribbon and pacifier turn up again, but no one mentions the money. When my wife checks the girls' homework it becomes obvious that only if a friend of ours keeps her promise to play and work with the two girls regularly are they able to more or less keep up with their schoolwork. But even if that works, will it be more than a drop of water on a hot stone?

By this time I have a better understanding of why my wife contradicted the speaker who claimed "everything foreign is an enrichment to us." She only protested in a whisper, for many bystanders perhaps would have misunderstood. Official pedagogical multiculturalism has as little use for subtleties as does the fear of strangers which such multiculturalism opposes. This kind of multiculturalism makes little of the communication barriers and renders them innocuous. Moreover, it often covers up its own tendency to invent the stereotypes with which we seek to orient ourselves in real life. Consequently, it tends to give insufficient consideration to both the opportunities and the difficulties of living with strangers.

Jews and Christians agree that the coexistence of people who are strangers to each other should be determined by the commandment to love. "You shall also love the stranger," Deuteronomy 10:19 says clearly. That commandment would be accepted quickly if we added, too eagerly, "love the stranger, *for he is like you.*" When associating with strangers—as when asso-ciating with the enemy—the meaning of love of neighbor be-comes clear, because strangers are different from us.

Love encourages acceptance of the other in his/her oth-erness. That is precisely why love has so often been denied to the stranger. Nevertheless, love can alter our personal attitudes. Can it also stamp coexistence on society? This question is being handled today under the rubric "multiculturalism."

It is true that this discussion has not so far landed on solid factual ground, for then one question could not be avoided: What are the elementary rules that must be acknowledged by everyone if diverse peoples are to live together?

The basic issue in our visits to the foreign families was al-ways the same one, though expressed differently. We had to ex-plain to them the rules that must be adhered to for the sake of coexistence. Some of these rules are undoubtedly peculiar to life in the German Federal Republic; for example, our particular work ethic and school attendance requirements. But are all of them limited to our culture? Is respect for the property of others a cultural peculiarity of West Europeans? Or are there some principles of justice that everyone could affirm without being forced to do so?

These experiences lead me very cautiously to my first con-clusion, namely that particular lifestyles can coexist in their variety only when agreement can be reached on elementary rules applicable to all. But reasons must be given as to why they do apply to all and why they can be affirmed voluntarily. Diversity within the realm of an ethic of the *good* is dependent on agreement on the ethic of the *just*. This insight of abstract moral theory can have practical application in real life.

INTERNAL DIVERSITY AND EXTERNAL BOUNDARIES

The tension between internal diversity and outward boundaries characterizes the histories of both the United States and Germany, each in their own ways. Both countries, a hodgepodge of different elements and peoples as few others are, have both had periods in their histories of extreme efforts to exclude strangers, eliminate outsiders, and establish homogeneity—often using murderous violence to achieve those ends.

This blending of peoples has been particularly difficult in considering German identity. Whenever the country has managed to find its way toward unification, difficulties in these matters have gotten out of hand. A national state is a state on the hunt for its enemies, and this is true both in Germany and in the United States. Defining oneself as against the enemy is the classic national state model for finding one's identity. In such cases, the task of politics essentially becomes the effort to distinguish friends from foes.

In Germany, the Bismarck empire established this pattern in its attempts to define itself in terms of what it opposed. In so doing, it gave rise to the problems of anti-Semitism, anti-Socialism, and the conflicts between the state and the Roman Catholic church. Lower middle-class persons, such as artisans and farmers, felt their livelihoods threatened as much by the capitalistic citizenry as by the Socialist workers. Hatred of whatever was alien helped them to compensate for their own sense of danger. They therefore steered their loyalty toward the nation and its political representatives, uniting themselves in their rejection of strangers.

Similar situations can be found in the United States. During the Cold War, the McCarthy hearings produced a witchhunt for suspected Communists. This search for enemies alienated major portions of the entire nation, ruining lives and squelching diversity of thought. Today debates over free trade and immigration policies push many to advocate for a "Fortress America" stance, promoting protectionism and xenophobic attitudes. One politician has gone so far as to call for the building of a wall along the southern border of the United States in order to keep out Mexicans and other illegal immigrants. America is becoming increasingly divided along ethnic, economic, and gender lines, with African American males becoming the country's largest "at-risk" population, and single mothers and homosexuals demonized as enemies of the family.

These historical precedents have their present-day counterparts. Enmity toward aliens, foreigners, and immigrants has grown with the unification of the Germany and the end of the Cold War. Yet those who stand against such intolerance and oppressive nationalisms are often motivated by attitudes not unlike those whom they oppose. It is not for nothing that those who claim to stand for inclusivity and "political correctness" are often referred to as the "thought police."

Can modern societies develop a reasonable and therefore complex identity? In Germany one must doubt that the answer to this question will be positive. Not only are right-wing extremists confronting foreigners with brutal, sometimes murderous violence, but this behavior—at least until the Heidelberg rally—could be sure to receive either quiet agreement or loud applause on the part of large segments of the German population. The escalating violence in America—especially that directed at tourists and exchange students—raises doubts whether the situation there is much more hopeful, but there are signs that grass roots groups composed of civic leaders and persons of varying political and religious persuasions, as well as of social and ethnic status, are coming together to find solutions.

No matter how much cynicism has played a role, two things have now become necessary. First, we must insist that racism and violence against foreigners have no place in our countries and we must use all legal means to achieve this.

Second, we can no longer postpone clarification of what kind of society we want. Do we want a homogeneous society in which the presence of strangers is merely tolerated as a necessary evil, or a culturally open society that continually reestablishes a consensus on the conditions of coexistence? The decision will not generally be made by the minorities newly arrived in the country, but by the majority that shapes the social climate.

MAJORITIES AND MINORITIES

The differentiation between majorities and minorities is itself questionable, for the status of minority is, most of the time, dictated and defined by the majority. Minorities are not accorded second-class status of their own volition. They are made "minorities" by the majority. True, this rule has one important exception: minorities that consider themselves the elite and lay claim to ruling others were not made so by the majority—they created themselves.

When analysed a bit more systematically, three basic types of majority and minorities are revealed. First, there is a middle-class elitist way of talking about majority and minority, adopted from the aristocratic models of the past. This model attributes to the majority a sober average quality above which rises the extraordinary achievement of an elitist minority. Members of this minority have an infallible instinct for recognizing each other, because they always float to the surface: "We are the blobs of fat floating in the nation's soup; we always bump into each other." They have an interest in having the majority remain as homogeneous as possible, kept unified through a binding national consciousness, common notions of morality, and a foundation of basic religious rites. The relationship between minority and majority is one of control.

Second, things are turned upside down when the concept of minority is based not in elitism one but simply in *discrimination*. In such cases minorities are those that do not adapt themselves to the norms of the majority's society. They stand out because of deviant behavior, strange customs, or unreliable morality. That it was the majority that defined this behavior as deviant was discovered by the sociologist Norbert Elias in 1960 in his study of a small city in England.[3] Elias showed that there is a configuration between majority and minorities, between insiders and outsiders, that functions this way: Insiders attribute universally to the outside group precisely those bad traits found in the most extreme members of the insider group, such as criminality and unreliability. Thus, those traits could be split off, and no longer be problems of their own group, but instead be ascribed to the strangers. At the same time, insiders build their self-image on the best traits in their own group—the ability to achieve, obedience to the law, and reliability—and then generalize those as characteristics of their own group as a whole. That is how the outsiders are turned into anomalous minorities, whereas the majority is seen as being thoroughly normal, oriented to the norm.

The double distortion (caricature) that results is particularly damnable because it is solidified with empirical evidence. It is never difficult to come up with illustrations proving that one's own group is good but the minority group is bad. For example, it is enough to report in detail about shoplifting by foreigners but fail to report shoplifting by natives. That is how to create the impression that the stereotype is reality.

Even when unprejudiced eyes observe that the structural difference between majority and minority is not that great, the majority's stereotypes make it appear great. Inequality before the law, or refusal to grant minorities the right to participate in politics, can therefore be easily justified. Highly potent stigmatizations are thus created without having to resort to long-term propaganda efforts. These stigmatizations are so effective precisely because they are accepted "innocently and naively"[4] by the establishment.

The relationship between majority and minority is determined by the image of normal and abnormal in the cases I have just described. This can lead, in extreme cases, to a majority seeing itself as deviating so greatly from society's prevailing norms that it labels itself a minority. This, as Simone De Beauvoir has demonstrated in her important book *The Second Sex*, is the fundamental experience of women in a male-dominated society. Elfriede Jelinek summarized this experience:

> Woman is the other, man is the norm. He has a place. . . . Woman has no place. With the glance of a speechless foreigner, Woman, the inhabitant of an alien planet, looks from outside into the reality in which she does not belong.[5]

The third way of talking about minorities, along with the elitist and the discriminatory, is the simple procedural way of classifying majorities and minorities by their numbers, and drawing conclusions on that basis.

The establishment of majority and minority is a democracy's authoritative process of decision. The decision, a fact often forgotten, rests on three decisive assumptions about the principle of majority: the first is that all voices have equal value and therefore the fundamental equality of all participants is recognized; second, that it is defensible and bearable only if there is a clearly limited area within which the majority can make decisions, and thus a sphere not applicable to majority vote is recognized; third, that the minority can become the majority and therefore has the right to revise earlier majority decisions.

This procedural model of looking at the relationship between majority and minority is rich in assumptions. It relies on the acknowledgment of elementary rules established in the interest of all participants—rules that can be approved by everyone with good reason. It is not cultural imperialism to insist that democracy rests on principles that can claim universal validity. Nor is it cultural imperialism to cling to these universal principles even when they conflict with the particular lifestyles of other cultures, for they also conflict with many aspects of our own culture, if we are honest enough to admit it. Nor can it be held against these principles that they were founded on the religious conviction that humans are created in the image of

God. If this conviction is true, then these principles are not limited to the adherents of the Abrahamic religions of Judaism, Christianity, and Islam.

To cling to these universal principles is necessary primarily because they alone can prevent an elitist minority from assuming rule over majorities, or an authoritarian majority from restricting or violating a minority's rights to exist.

On the basis of our short discussion of the rules of behavior in a democracy, we can establish these four principles: (1) equal respect for all human beings; (2) protection of basic rights, which the majority has no right to control; (3) respect for the plurality of groups with differing convictions and lifestyles; and (4) nonviolence when dealing with social conflicts, particularly social conflicts on matters of truth.

First and foremost, a procedural understanding of the relation of majority to minorities commits one to question the static mindset of the majority society. Under the conditions of democracy, the identity of a society can no longer be considered the sure property of the majority. Instead, creating this identity should be understood as a project dependent on the cooperation of diverse minorities. In these advanced modern circumstances, no society any longer forms a homogeneous unity whose continuity is guaranteed by the reliability of traditions. Moreover, the unity of the society is constantly being reestablished. Traditions are not inherited guarantors of unity but rather are constructively introduced in the process of finding unity.

MULTICULTURALISM

In the struggle for the future of our society, the issue is whether we want to orient ourselves to the image of a homogeneous ethnic state or to an open republic guided by human rights. The "open republic" model has often been discussed under the rubric of multiculturalism. Can multiculturalism describe a society in which the majority respects the dignity and rights of the minorities, and in which the minorities have space for their own equal lifestyle?

In the debate of the last few years, objections were raised which had their origin in various views of multiculturalism. Frank-Olaf Radke has distinguished three types of thinking on multiculturalism, and sharply criticized each: the programatic-pedagogical, the culinary-cynical, and the demographic-instrumental.

Programatic-pedagogical multiculturalism claims that the politically ideal image is that of the multicultural society, and that the key theme of emancipated pedagogy is the teaching of multicultural coexistence. It often tends to be romantically blind regarding contradictions in society and takes on a moralistic tone. As a result its proponents are more concerned with the hygiene of their own souls than with the minorities, on whom they then make demands.

Culinary-cynical multiculturalism places what alien cultural lifestyles offer at the service of individual appreciation of the good life. Chinese or Afghan restaurants are in great demand, but no attention is paid to the living conditions of the Chinese or Afghans in the host country. This type of multicultural thinking serves the cultural enrichment of the "winners of modernization," namely those who have profited from the increased choices of individual lifestyles in the process of social modernization. The offerings of alien kitchens and cultures are exploited by those who themselves have no worries about the future, and who cynically make use of the new interest in regional culinary specialties and ethnic differences.

Demographic-instrumental multiculturalism starts with the fact that a highly industrial society, wherein the birthrate is lower than the death rate, cannot survive in the long run without immigration. Its principal intent is to correct the pyramid of old age by importing younger members of society capable of working and paying into Social Security. The living conditions of immigrants is, from this viewpoint, of secondary importance to the demand for regulated immigration to fill existing needs.

The ambivalence of all three types is obvious. Yet they under-estimate the critical, clarifying potential contained in the con-cept of multiculturalism. This potential is revealed only when a careful distinction is made between two levels on which the problem of multiculturalism rests. One level is the *descrip-tion* of a multicultural reality, the other is the *structure* of that reality.

On the first level, multiculturalism reveals the fact that vari-ous distinct cultural imprints exist within the one and same so-cial context. We are faced with the fact that we are dealing with a form of social pluralism which by far surpasses the variations contained within the same culture. This description holds true even when we have to object to today's frequent overemphasis on ethnic differences, and becomes even more accurate to the degree that it realistically notes the conflicts arising out of these coexisting differences.

On a second level, however, multiculturalism signifies more than this kind of description. It signifies the reasoned and con-scious affirmation of diversity. Multiculturalism does not yet ex-ist, in the sense that the side-by-side life of different cultures is accepted as inevitable in time and durability. One can speak of that only when the intentional encounter and exchange be-tween the various cultures is encouraged and arranged.

Multiculturalism is not only a descriptive term, it is a pro-gramatic concept. Beate Winkler sketched its programatic meaning in this way:

> Multicultural society means: majority and minority coexist with equality in mutual respect and with tolerance for the different culturally formed attitudes and modes of behavior of the other.[6]

ACKNOWLEDGING THE STRANGER AND ONE'S OWN IDENTITY

Multiculturalism, understood in this way, rests on two im-portant assumptions: on mutual acknowledgment and on per-ceived identity.

First, multiculturalism rests on mutual acknowledgment. It can unfold only where the existence and the rights of other cultures are respected. Respect for human dignity in the person of strangers, tolerance for their way of life, and nonviolence when participating in a conflict between different claims to truth, are decisive conditions not only for the pluralistic society as a whole but for the multicultural society as well.

A multicultural society is founded on an understanding reached regarding the elementary rules of a society based on law, which makes mutual acknowledgment possible and secures it. These rules themselves cannot be established capriciously in the name of multiculturalism. Instead, the cultures must arrive at a consensus regarding them. Since understanding is transmitted through language, one of the conditions for multiculturalism must be learning the language of the country.

An important theme for multicultural coexistence is therefore a discussion about key values. These "core values" are perceived and formulated differently in the different cultural traditions, but they do meet in intersecting areas. To be sure, this demand for "core values" can be used to sabotage multiculturalism. The content of these rules can be shaped in such a way that what is demanded is a complete, exclusive worldview, and they can also be so closely tied to specific religious or cultural backgrounds that they lose every vestige of reasonable openness. If only to prevent such dangers, every formulation of unconditional social consensus must always remain open to revision. It bears a historical character open to reason and revision simultaneously.

The fundamental experience of developing "core values" is part of the development of modern democracy, particularly in its formulation of human rights. Democracy certainly does not owe its existence to a homogeneous cultural background. Instead, it is the result of processes of differentiation, in which no specific cultural or even religious imprint could call the tune.

To claim that democracy is a child of Christianity, as has sometimes occurred recently, really does require a large measure of historical brashness. Although an undoubted resemblance exists between the basic ideas of a democracy and the Christian understanding of humanity, the constitutional form of a democracy could succeed only once the large Christian churches' claim to a monopoly on transmitting social meaning had given way to a plurality of life orientations. When viewed more closely, then, modern democracy is a consequence of the separation between Christian confessions as well as the growing differentiation between religious and secular ways of life.

Overcoming religious, cultural, and political conflicts, a minimal democratic consensus was formed that encompassed a specific image of humanity. It views human persons, in the formulation of the American philosopher of law John Rawls, as "free and equal . . . capable of sensible and rational behavior and so of participation in social cooperation with other persons like them." [7]

This minimal consensus on human rights anchors its view of humanity in the notion of the equal value of all persons, out of which follow the basic elements of a secure legal position in society. Nor is this minimal consensus on human rights exclusively bound to a particular cultural tradition, that of Christianity and the Enlightenment. It is, in principle, open to reason. Nevertheless, the common element at all levels of the unfolding and codification of human rights to the present day is the goal of safeguarding the equal worth of all in their variety. The minimal consensus becomes open to doubt when, on the basis of race, gender, sexual orientation, religion, or political preference people are discriminated against, physically injured, or excluded from the chance to develop.

The declaration of equal human rights also forms the fixed point for the program of multiculturalism. That is why Beate Winkler demands in the German context, "Multicultural society must always measure itself, in its way of life, by . . . the equality commandment [of the Constitution]." [8]

Nor, for a community based on law, is it a violation of the fundamental rules of multiculturalism but rather a necessary subject of agreement regarding minimal conditions when, for example, the society views the surgical removal of Arab girls' clitorises as a violation of their physical integrity and therefore questions the practice, or when it rejects the demand for legal acknowledgment of polygamy on the ground that this way of life is based on systematic discrimination against women.

Both the necessity for, and the difficulties of, a consensus on the elementary rules for a community based on law are revealed in exemplary manner in the development of human rights. For one thing, multiculturalism needs to acknowledge strangers. For another, it must be based on the presence and further development of diverse specific identities. No multiculturalism can be established where particular cultural imprints are not consciously recognized and nurtured, made into traditions and developed further, reflected upon and altered. Cultural exchange presupposes cultural particularities.

This applies to the religious realm as well. Interreligious dialogues depend on the fact that the religion of the participants is a way of life to them. Christian faith contributes to multiculturalism only when it retains its credibility as Christian faith. Theology supports the development of multiculturalism when it remains true to the particular truth it needs to interpret. Theological theories about religion fail to encourage multiculturalism precisely when they stress only the common elements in the various religions without at the same time investigating what is specific to each.

To this extent, multiculturalism is a counternotion and a counterproposal to the relativism so often hidden behind the use of this term. It is also a counternotion and counterproposal to the kind of individualizing of lifestyles that considers everything one could think of to be equally valid and therefore equally acceptable. The exchange between cultures presupposes their differentiation. Only those who can name their differences can seek what binds cultures together.

The concept of multiculturalism is vulnerable not only to being misunderstood but also to being abused. It is abused in the same way that the concept of culture in general is abused. The widespread understanding of culture is that it is a social system of component parts, and so the structural crises of the modern age are not blamed on the economic but rather on the cultural system of component parts.

Much of this understanding can be attributed to the Zürich philosopher Hermann Lübbe, who thinks the economic crisis of the modern industrial society is not one of goals but solely a navigational crisis which becomes apparent only if it is recognized as a crisis in cultural orientation. "The future of modern industrialized society does not ultimately depend on economic factors but rather on cultural and moral factors."[9]

This kind of observation renders the extent of the economic cause of the present crisis innocuous, and overtaxes culture, resulting in extreme claims. Thus Lübbe not only calls for the expansion of cultural tradition for the sake of a particular cultural identity but also—much more pointedly and not coincidentally in the language of security—for "securing our national and regional forms of imprinted origins."[10] That is certainly a demand that renders a reasoned concept of culture indistinguishable from ethnic folk tradition.

If multiculturalism is to be understood as the present society's guide to the society of the future, then the concept must be protected against the misinterpretations mentioned above, just as much as against the abuse that blames culture for the problems that can only be solved by reforming the economy. I believe that only then does the concept of a multicultural society have a productive meaning.

THE OFFER OF SUCCESSFUL MULTICULTURALISM

The concept of multiculturalism precisely defined can be endowed with an orienting quality, not in an exclusive, but rather in an inclusive, sense. For many reasons, it mirrors a fundamental ethical intuition very clearly expressed in the history of

Judaism and Christianity. In contradistinction to long dominant traits of Christian history, it pays to consider the more basic elements of Jewish and Christian tradition, which reveal a noticeable correspondence to the composition of a multicultural society.

Not only the Greek New Testament, but also the Hebrew Bible—the Old Testament for Christians—already accept to good advantage what alien cultures offer. Israel's creation notions go back to even more ancient traditions, for biblical prehistory already recognized the cultural prominence of other peoples. First and foremost, Israel does not, as do the creation myths of other cultures, describe the first human beings as members of their own people, but rather—in the duality of man and woman—as images of God. As a result, the Old Testament notions of human beings possess a fundamental characteristic that opposes discrimination against, and marginalization of, individuals as well as minority groups.

The basic experience of Israel can be described as liberation from unsuccessful multiculturalism. Their opportunities in Egypt were destroyed by the claims to power on the part of the native ruling classes. Departure—exodus—was the response, which was experienced as the gift of freedom, and became known as such. Out of this experience, Israel's concept of law particularly accents the rights of aliens. Their own experience in exile was always cited as explanation: "You shall not wrong or oppress a resident alien, for you were aliens in the land of Egypt" (Exod. 22:21). Dealing with aliens is where the structure of neighborly love is revealed: "But you shall love your neighbor as yourself: I am the LORD" (Lev. 19:18).

The Old Testament laws and their interpretation in the Talmud are not content to rank aliens in accordance with the law of hospitality that attempts to attain a balance between the interests of host and guest. Instead, out of God's love of the stranger comes the unconditional devotion to the alien neighbor as a fundamental moral duty pointing beyond the calculations involved in weighing various interests. The Jewish philos-

opher Herman Cohen already formulated the insight in 1888—
at a time of inflamed anti-Semitism—that love of neighbor
(more precisely, love of the nationality and faith of aliens), is a
commandment that Judaism introduced into the development
of moral ideas.

This fundamental theme continues strongly in Jesus' proclamation. He once again emphasized that love of enemy is called
an exemplary case of love of neighbor (Matt. 5:43–48). But that
basic theme is also revealed when Jesus equates rejection of the
stranger with rejection of himself (Matt. 25:43; cf. 25:35).

At this point acknowledgment of the stranger really seems to
be a basic condition of Christian life praxis. It encompasses
both respecting the otherness of the other but maintaining
one's right to one's own homeland.

Under the limited conditions of communities of faith in a
pagan environment, the early Christian congregations already
developed structures for mutual acknowledgment of others
who were different. Paul's paradoxical formula that there is no
longer Jew nor Greek, no longer slave nor free, no longer male
and female (Gal. 3:28), if seen close up, contains the proposal
that, in light of the joint membership in the body of Christ,
irrevocable differences be relativized in such a way that these
differences become not only bearable but advantageous and
constructive. This is demonstrated fully in Paul's teaching about
the gifts of grace—the charisms—to the community in 1 Corin-
thians 12. This passage declares the differences among the
members of the congregation to be necessary for the sake of
the community.

Christians today discover the truth of these early insights in
extremely different contexts. These insights had their deepest
roots in Israel's liberation experiences as well as those of Chris-
tendom. These experiences of liberation pointed out God's par-
tisanship toward the alienated, those who had been made, or
had become, strangers. There are profound reasons for the fact
that not only the phenomenon of the *other* but also that of the
stranger have suddenly aroused the interest of modern theolo-

gians, and that some theologians have called for a theological "hermeneutic of the stranger."

Let me put forward one element of this "hermeneutic of the stranger." Today's debates about multiculturalism tend to categorize groups by stereotypes. This kind of stereotyping can come up not only in the form of images of the enemy but also in images of friend. The friend-image also lets the person— the unique, single individual—be submerged in the collective. The generalities we use in talking of Serbs or Croats, of Kurds or Iraqis, of Mexicans or Japanese, bear many aspects of stereotype.

Yet every human being hopes to remain differentiated from these solidified images. We all know the relief we feel when a stranger who has come to know us better tells us we are not "typical" of our peculiar national, sexual, or regional identity. Differentiating the person from the image, from the collective stereotype we have constructed, is one of the contributions the Christian faith must make toward thinking about multiculturalism.

This differentiation can be linked to the Reformation interpretation of the justification of human beings before God. That interpretation reminds us that no human person is ultimately defined by the sum of his/her actions. Rather, God accepts the person independently of that person's works, with the result, however, that no other individual or social institution has the right to equate that person with his/her works.

The dignity of every person is to be respected, independent of all merit or fault. Therefore, for the coexistence of human beings, the most important consequence of our understanding of justification is the differentiation between persons and their deeds. The analogy is equally valid, that for a multicultural society the most important consequence drawn from justification thinking is the differentiation between persons and their cultural affiliation. Multicultural thinking is distinguished precisely through its refusal to have either foe or friend stereotypes dominate its perception of strangers.

When reflecting on the conditions of multiculturalism, their importance in the insights anchored in the history of Judaism and Christianity is obvious. But they appear in a form that allows us to recognize their passage through the experience of the Enlightenment. It was the Enlightenment that so universalized the Judaic/Christian talk of all human beings in God's image that it was incorporated—without its religious connotations—into the concept of human dignity. Thus, thinking about conditions for multiculturalism exemplifies that the insight into basic moral content has been preserved even under the circumstances of modernity.

The thesis by the American philosopher Alasdair MacIntyre that the process of the Enlightenment was gained at the necessary cost of the loss of virtue does not hold water. The hope of successful coexistence of people who are strangers to each other has not yet been doomed to failure.

COEXISTENCE IN CULTURAL DIVERSITY

If coexistence with strangers is to be learned, three conditions essential to that learning must be present:

First, readiness to coexist with strangers is developed by positive examples. This readiness is not brought about by condemning those who fear strangers.

In order to reduce prejudice, joint projects between Germans and Turks, Americans and Mexicans, Christians and Muslims, should be undertaken. Prejudice will not be reduced by simply moaning about hostility to strangers. A community of different people will be established only when the reasons for widespread fear are recognized and when one fights to eliminate these reasons rather than their consequences. One of the most frequent reasons is fear of social decline. Whoever fears unemployment or scarcity of housing will first of all try to chase out the foreigners who are possible rivals for employment or housing. Those who are not satisfied with snobbish prejudices but instead concern themselves with their causes will take effective and dangerous hostility toward strangers seriously.

Second, cultural foe-images appear quickly and are hard to erase. Cultural friendship is established more slowly but can become deeply rooted.

For many people, the Gulf War came at just the right time. The enemy-image of Soviet Communism that had been lost could now be replaced promptly with the enemy-image of Iraq and Saddam Hussein. I quote, as an example, the official German government "Information for the Troops," which viewed Islamic fundamentalism as the sole and only cause of the "World Civil War."

> It is directed . . . against the foundation of Western civilization and culture. We are all challenged, through this confrontation between Western Christian/Jewish civilization and Eastern Islamic fundamentalism.[11]

This is the way stereotypes are developed and nurtured, stereotypes that create great obstacles to the coexistence of diverse people. Whoever wishes to oppose such foe-images must obviously work on two levels at once. One needs concrete projects in places where people have the chance to get to know each other instead of talking about each other. But one also needs to work for a political culture that is not dependent on cliched foe-images. A mature democracy is distinguished by not viewing strangers as enemies.

Third, only someone interested in both alien cultures and his or her own cultural identity can contribute to a society of cultural diversity.

Two contradictory responses are often given to the de facto plurality of our society, both of which are unsatisfactory and indeed ominous. *Fundamentalism* wants a return to simple circumstances. It evades questions caused by oddities. It insists a small number of simple precepts should suffice to guide us through life. All else is ignored or rejected. This kind of fundamentalism exists not just in Islam, but also in Judaism

and Christianity. It exists in nonreligious people. It exists not
only in the political right but also in the political left. Fundamentalism seals itself off from possible truth, possible values,
the richness within a person, and the experience, faith, and culture of the other, the stranger. That is why its intolerance is
inhuman.

Opposing fundamentalism is *relativism,* which states that every human being has his or her own convictions and lifestyle
and no understanding is possible in any case. We do not proceed with the challenging truth so important to us as individuals when we meet others. According to this model, the variety
of people and groups can live well together because they are
ultimately indifferent to each other. Relativism states that a plu-
ralized society can only exist by no longer asking the serious,
deep questions important to humans and by making the answers to these questions taboo. This kind of multiculturalism
ultimately ends with the death of all culture.

Whoever works for a society oriented to the dignity of all has
a different goal today: The goal of a culturally open society in
which all people of good will can find a home; a society capable
of achieving peace, in the inner core of which there exists a
peace between different people that we also hope to achieve
between nations; a society oriented toward human rights in
which the rights of minorities enjoy particular protection and
concern.

Work for a culturally open, peaceable society oriented toward
human rights is proving to be more difficult and to move more
slowly than many people had hoped even a short time ago. In
Germany, for instance the "immigration of fear for the future"
(Beate Winkler) is stronger than these people wanted to admit.
The situation has been aggravated by employing political tac-
tics to create delays and mark time, by refusing to implement
simple measures legally provided for already, by conducting abstract discussions about changes in the constitution instead of
taking practical action, and by exploiting foreigners as pawns
for various interest groups. It is still doubtful whether hu-

maneness and political sanity will be able to gain the upper hand on this issue. Yet alertness and persistence remain advisable even when there is success in regulating the asylum law and the problems of migration and immigration are dealt with in a way concomitant with human rights.

Is there a lesson to be learned from the experiences strangers have had in dealing with us Germans after unification fell on us? That lesson probably consists first and foremost in the members of the majority society learning to look at themselves through the eyes of others. If this succeeds, there is still hope for a better Germany, and a better world.

CHAPTER FOUR

A Look Back at the Gulf War

On August 2, 1990, Iraqi armed forces attacked Kuwait and occupied it. After failing in the Iraq-Iran War (1979–1988) to establish Iraq as the leading power in the Persian Gulf, Saddam Hussein now made a second attempt. The roots of the conflict date back to the time of British colonial rule, for Iraq had questioned the Kuwait border when Kuwait obtained its total independence in 1961. Moreover, the war against Iran had increased Iraq's debt. The immense expenses of Saddam's tyrannical dictatorship and concomitant economic depression, as well as the conflict over the price of oil, drove his regime into a corner. Saddam planned to use military force to get rid of his debts by dominating Kuwait and the other rich Gulf states, which, through OPEC, had set quotas on production to enforce high oil prices. He was totally indifferent to the right of the neighboring countries to self-determination.

The conflict could not possibly be confined to the region. Its global character became apparent to all when the first U.S. soldiers landed in Saudi Arabia on August 8, 1990. The various stages of the conflict were marked by the U.N. Security Council Resolutions (although this does not mean that the United Nations had the script in hand). The starring role the United States assumed was manifest not just in its commanding position in the military alliance gathered to oppose Iraq, but also in the economic boycott imposed on Iraq.

This boycott was carried out half-heartedly and lost a great deal of its possible effectiveness due to a problematic ultimatum: On November 29, 1990, the U.N. Security Council delivered to Iraq the ultimatum to remove its troops unconditionally from Kuwait by January 15, 1991. Saddam Hussein refused. "Operation Desert Storm" was launched during the night of January 17, 1991. Two of the U.S.-led alliance's three goals were achieved within a very short time: First, Kuwait was liberated, and, second, Iraq was robbed of a large portion of its military and technical potential. But the third goal—the termination of Saddam's rule of Iraq—failed. Iraq's suppression of Kurdish and Shiite resistance continued and even intensified.

Some people soon declared this war to have been unavoidable and supported their view by asserting that Saddam had forced the failure of any peace policy: "No policy, no matter how clever, no matter how tactful, could deal with a foe like that. He will ultimately always get what he wants . . . war.[1] For others, the Gulf War was one more example of "organized brutality's successful perversion into moral action."[2]

Some called for supporting the American-led alliance, either branding every other opinion as anti-Americanism, or demanding military protection for Israel's right to exist, seeing every other opinion as a dire forgetting of Israel, if not outright anti-Semitism. Others insisted that war was not a responsible method to resolve political conflicts in this case, and demanded "peace in the Gulf." When a truce was declared, the supporters lamented that the war had not lasted long enough, since "Hitler's successor" was still in power and Israel was still in danger. The others grieved over the victims of a short but brutal war and the long-lasting destruction.

The controversies over these events were never really resolved. Soon after the spring of 1991, the discussion waned, and by the summer of that year, it was carried on only in isolated situations. The desire to know more accurately what had happened and how to evaluate it was not widespread. Such disinterest is probably typical for a war widely viewed by the public as a television event.

Although the Gulf War was staged as a media event—"Just think, there is a war and the TV set is broken!"—we know very little about it. This is partly our own fault, but we are also partly victims of an enormous amount of censorship regarding the truth. No matter how much the events, as well as the consequences, are suppressed, a few indisputable results are apparent. The "Document on Peace 1991" by the three German Institutes for Peace Research formulated these results:

> Although the Gulf War solved the acute problem of the annexation of Kuwait and Iraq's threat to the region, it simultaneously gave rise to a series of grave new problems. Reconstruction of the once-modern nations of Iraq and Kuwait will take decades, and entail billions of petrodollars. The ecological consequence of oil pollution and oil fires in the Gulf are terrible. New streams of refugees—foreign workers, Iraqi Kurds, and Shiites—put a burden on the region. Saddam Hussein is solidly in power, and a peaceful resolution of the Iraqi civil war is not in sight.[3]

The satisfaction of the belligerent faction—those who considered this war inevitable—as well as the alarm of the pacifists about this war, were quickly suppressed over the course of 1991; soon other events overshadowed these feelings. This media event disappeared as quickly as it had appeared. As passionately as the intellectuals had debated before, so silent did they soon become. As vehemently as arguments based on the just war doctrine had taken place in the church, so quickly were they now stilled.

These necessary concerns were never clarified. Alarm over the Gulf War was silenced by the apparent military success and was pushed aside by another war even more confusing to people, the war in the Balkans. It is therefore important to swim against the current of forgetfulness and to keep in mind some questions the Gulf War has raised.

MAY WAR BE GOD'S WILL?

The sentence "War is not allowed according to God's will" was repeated in many prayers for peace in 1991. Later many doubted that that prayer was justified. This prayer seems to quote from the first plenary session of the Ecumenical Council of Churches in Amsterdam in 1948. The formulation there was not exactly "War is not allowed according to God's will"; it was, more precisely, "War *must not be,* according to God's will." [4]

The statement that war is not *allowed* leads to the conclusion that what is not allowed cannot be. But the statement that war *must* not be stresses the task of political responsibility, which provides common ground on which adherents of diverse traditions of peace ethics can meet. The duty to prevent with all one's might any recourse to the murderous violence of war unites diverse ethical positions on peace. It applies to the proponents of the principle of pacifism as well as adherents to the just war doctrine.

This duty is not nullified by the fact that a superior military force was able to use force to accomplish one part of its goals. The fact that war can be waged does not nullify the duty to prevent it.

Nor is it an accurate thesis that the Gulf War demonstrated, even in this day of potential mass destruction, that it is still possible to wage war on a limited scale. Although it is true that no war since World War II, except the Korean War and the Vietnam War, has aroused as much worldwide attention as the Gulf War of 1991, the number of wars in the world since 1945 is depressing proof that there has been no interruption in waging war. It did not have to be proved by the military action in the Gulf.

Wars were also being waged during the time that we avoided an outbreak of military conflict between the superpowers and their allies through the exchange of mutual threats. Depending on the method of counting, the number of these wars after 1945 is between 150 and 190. For the period between mid-1990 and 1991 alone, forty-four wars were being waged in the world. Nor is war eliminated automatically. It disappears only to the extent in which work is done to eliminate the causes of political tension and efforts are made to find mechanisms for nonmilitary solutions to conflicts.

IS THERE SUCH A THING AS INEVITABLE WAR?

"War must not be, according to God's will." This statement has an unequivocal meaning in the biblical confession to the God who, as creator of life, is also a lover of all living things (see Prov. 11:24–12:1). Yet this does not exclude the possibility of having situations in which the use of force is inevitable. Where life is attacked or destroyed or where no other means is available to counter threatened violence, loyalty to the lover of all living things can also include the temptation to use Beelzebub to drive out the devil.

It is not just individuals who appropriate unavoidable guilt through their behavior, as Dietrich Bonhoeffer did by participating in the conspiracy against Hitler. The appropriation of unavoidable guilt also exists in the behavior of political organisms; it is present when the death of human beings is tolerated in the course of police actions against criminals or terrorists.

We frequently forget that guilt is appropriated in these cases as well. The language used in the churches to present the just war doctrine encouraged such forgetfulness. Those who "justify" the policeman's fatal shot, the refusal to accede to the terrorists' death threat, or the use of violence in war, and who therefore label this kind of behavior "just" in some situations, cover up the severity of the ethical conflict. This conflict occurs because responsibility to our own life or that of a stranger requires us to act in such a way as damages our responsibility to life in general. The balancing of the good achieved does not resolve the conflict, since life cannot be balanced against life. In such situations, responsibility requires from us a balancing of guilt.

Was labeling the Gulf War "terribly necessary" a balancing of guilt? Such a judgment means that the warlike use of force as a "means of last resort (*ultima ratio*)" was inevitable.

This kind of judgment—overtly or not—makes use of the just war doctrine, which for hundreds of years was of decisive importance in Christian judgments on issues of war and peace. This doctrine starts with the primacy of peace over war—a fact frequently forgotten. It intends, even when all too often it is used in opposition to its original sense, to establish criteria for when the ultimate means of warlike force may be used and which of these means can be accounted justified. In other words, this doctrine intends to differentiate just from unjust wars and justifiable from unjustifiable means of waging war.

In the course of time and the complex development of the doctrine, seven criteria to support this intention were formulated:

(1) There must be a just reason for war, primarily a violent attack from the other side, which requires defense.
(2) The war is a means of last resort to reestablish peace.
(3) It must be waged and explained by a political authority empowered to do so.
(4) The war must be waged with peace as the goal.
(5) There must be a reasonable prospect for successful termination of the war.
(6) The appropriateness of the means must not be exceeded.
(7) The commandment to differentiate combatants from noncombatants, and therefore the immunity of the civilian population, must not be violated.

The first and the fifth criteria were honored in the Gulf War, because Iraq had broken the law and disturbed the peace by occupying Kuwait. And the allies so waged the war that a successful termination of war in the foreseeable future proved feasible. Was the war thus "terribly necessary"? That judgment leads one astray, since the war was extremely problematic in view of the other five criteria. Therefore a positive verdict would be justified by the just war doctrine only if:

- All other means of resolving the Kuwait crisis had been exhausted.
- The military measures undertaken against Iraq had been carried out by an international entity legally commissioned to do so.
- These measures had been aimed at establishing peace in the Middle East in a recognizable and convincing manner.
- The means employed had been appropriate to the requirements.
- The measures taken had been aimed at sparing the civilian population and civilian targets.

The Gulf War cannot be deemed "terribly necessary" by those criteria. That would have required above all that all other means to end the conflict had been exhausted. But the means of economic and political pressure expressly foreseen by the Charter of the United Nations were not carried out to the end. Moreover, every interpretation of the war that would explain it on the basis of pursuing the economic interests of the rich industrial nations would have to have been precluded. But to preclude that interpretation, the most powerful industrial nation should not have assumed supreme command of the armed forces. And the United States could by no means claim it was carrying out the orders of the United Nations in accordance with the U.N. Charter. Consequently, the second and third criteria in particular were not fulfilled.

I do not want to overplay the discordant elements of the just war doctrine when I apply these criteria. The discordance is contained first and foremost in its tendency to render the use of violence innocuous by viewing it as "justifiable." This tendency has been reinforced recently when all the warring parties declare their own war "just."

No less important is how this way of thinking renders innocuous the problem of justice. One abstracts an isolated action
out of the larger, interwoven story of injustice and declares that
to be the sole cause of the war. The American ethicists Alan
Geyer and Barbara Green have compared this kind of judgment
to the behavior of a football referee who penalizes a team's action without taking into account the foul that preceded it. As a
rule, all participants in a war contribute to that war's injustice.

But above all, the just war doctrine separates justice from
love; it contains no opening for the possibility of reconciliation,
no chance for a new beginning. Principled pacifism's rebuttal is
thus indispensable, because it interrupts the closed system of
thinking about injustice and retaliation.

Despite this discordance, the just war doctrine, applied in its
original critical sense, is an aid to ethical judgments. The doctrine as yet has not been replaced in its specific function by any
more practical proposal. If one applies it to the Gulf War, the
doctrine's verdict is negative. The Gulf War cannot be declared
a "just war."

However, another verdict could be reached when one considers the threat to Israel's existence posed by Iraq's policy and
military potential. In that respect, Konrad Weiss correctly stated
that it would be too simple and too easy "to demand peace
from a secure distance and to deny someone else the right of
self defense." For that reason I myself declared, while the Gulf
War was still being waged, that Germany could not refuse to
offer defensive weapons to Israel. I added,

> We must confess that we have not taken seriously enough our
> responsibility with regard to a permanent peace in the Middle
> East which includes the Palestinians as well as the Israelis. . . .
> The people in whose name and with whose hands the genocide
> of European Judaism was carried out is by guilt tied to an Israel
> in new danger through a dictator who announces emphatically
> that he will not hesitate to use weapons of mass destruction. It
> is now our obvious duty to participate in the protection of Israel.

But the dutiful acknowledgment of Israel's right to exist and
taking on the duty to protect it did not render "Desert Storm"

inevitable. Instead, this action increased the immediate danger to Israel. The destruction of the Iraqi military potential and the imposition of severe conditions for truce created a breathing space for Israel but not much more. It is still valid to say that Israel's right to exist will in the long run be secured permanently only when the Palestinians' right to exist is included in the framework of a comprehensive peace for the region. The failure to accomplish this policy was not cancelled out by the Gulf War nor achieved through recent peace accords.

ARE THERE WORSE THINGS THAN WAR?

In my eyes, to derive a justification for the war from the danger to Israel is wrong. Prominent German historians did present an unfortunate justification along those lines. They explained that Iraq's military potential had to be destroyed so that the threat to Israel's existence would cease. They underlined that point by drawing a parallel to the genocide of European Jews that ended with the allies' victory over Germany. The murder of the Jewish people, so they said, was "ended solely by the willingness of the Americans, English, Russians, and others to wage war." They concluded, "Since Auschwitz, everyone must know that there are possibly worse things than war."

These words bring to mind the controversy between historians in 1986 and 1987, when some historians relativized the cruelty of Auschwitz by comparing it to other state crimes committed in our century. The historians who now spoke up in defense of the Gulf War had made important contributions to settling the 1986 controversy. That they did not stay true to their own insights is all the more terrible, for they now presented a change of front no less deplorable than relativizing Auschwitz. By what right did they—in comparing it with the unequaled "Shoah [holocaust]"—relativize the horrors of *any* war? By what right should we count the victims of German warfare against the Soviet Union—I don't even want to talk about their number!—as less important than the victims of German murderers in Auschwitz?

Every calculation of that sort runs counter to the insight that no reason, no matter how just it may be, can justify the murderous violence of war weapons. The goal of a war does not justify that war. One is reminded direfully of the statement of Alexander Haig—the American general who soon afterwards lost his bid for the presidential election—who said there were more important things than peace.

WHAT IS THE ROLE OF RELIGION?

When George Bush told his compatriots on January 17, 1991, that America was waging a just war against Iraq, he closed with a prayer on behalf of the soldiers, their families, and the American nation. And when, after six weeks, he announced the truce in the Persian Gulf, his last words were, "Good night, and may God protect the United States of America."

For his part, Saddam Hussein had already announced the invasion of Kuwait on August 2, 1990, "In the name of Allah, the Gracious and Merciful" and he later called upon Allah's help for "indisputable victory" over "Satan Bush."

These quotations demonstrate the detrimental role of religion in this war as well as the harmful role of this conflict in the dialogue between religions.

The Iraqi dictator succeeded in winning the support of a part of the Iraqi people for his violation of international law in invading Kuwait and for his terrible violation of human rights against the Kurdish people by making a coldblooded appeal to the fundamentalist emotions of pious Muslims. President Bush laid claim not only to God's blessing but also to the tradition of "just war" for his waging of war.

As a result, both American and European Christian groups explained that disagreeing with the war was necessary and commanded by Christ, and thousands demonstrated in the streets and city squares in support of that position. Some Jewish citizens, for their part, explained that the problem with the Gulf War was not that it had started but that it had ended too soon.

The truce should not have been declared until the Iraqi military potential had been totally destroyed and Saddam Hussein had been stripped of all power.

The terrible fate of the Kurds and the continued instability in the Middle East are points favoring the Israeli position. But one cannot deny that the opposing viewpoint also has justice on its side when it states that the use of weapons does not bring peace but rather creates new violence. A lasting peace can be achieved only by political means, not by military force.

OPPOSING OPTIONS IN THE ISSUE OF WAR AND PEACE

The issue of the relationship of the world religions to peace is full of pitfalls, as the example of the Gulf conflict shows. I will use this conflict as the occasion to characterize the main types of religious responses to the problem of war and peace.

The picture appears confusing at first. Contradictory opinions rain in on us, all of them equipped with religious justifications. All the religions claim that their doctrines and their praxis advance peace, which, of course, is open to contradictory interpretations, for the debate is over what peace is and what serves peace. Some see peace only as an interruption of war, others see peace as the fruit of justice. The first consider the readiness to take up arms if needed as the most important service to peace. The others believe that peace can grow only where people renounce all violence.

These different opinions and convictions are not necessarily allotted to different belief systems. They can show up within the same religion, within the same church. Protestantism, especially, harbors within itself contradictory notions of what peace is and what can lead to peace.

The Lutheran churches present the clearest example of a religious community in which contradictory notions of peace exist side by side and are repeatedly fought over. Freedom, the particular mark of Protestant Christianity, is demonstrated by the fact that no church authority can declare a specific form of political ethic doctrinally binding. Nor can it impose such an ethic by force. Instead, various ideas compete with each other, and this competition cannot be terminated by a word of command. The only way is the persistent search for common understanding.

Only experience, theological testing, and the power of a better argument can lead, step by step, to resolutions always debated anew. That is why different positions can be clearly formulated within Protestantism. And that is why I will use Protestantism to illustrate the four most important religious responses to the issue of war and peace. I call them "belligerence," "realism," "principled pacifism," and "responsible pacifism."

Belligerence

"Belligerence," or, to put it bluntly, the bent toward war, is my label for the notion that the use of military means is an acceptable and in many cases even the best way to solve international conflicts. Belligerence accepts not only defensive war but aggressive war as well. It is often combined with the view that history is a continuous fight of all against all. This view expands the claim of Charles Darwin regarding the biological evolution of the species with a social Darwinist very näive application to human history, in which only the strong can survive. Consequently, military strength and using this strength is a part of the historical vocation of a people that does not want to die out.

Such a bent toward war can be combined not only with social Darwinism but also with religious motives, which has frequently occurred in Protestantism. One example is a poem by the Lutheran pastor Dietrich Vorwerk, published at the beginning of World War I, entitled "Hurrah and Hallelujah," which copied part of the Lord's Prayer:

> Even if wretched the bread of war
> Give us this day the death of foes

Their tenfold pains!
In merciful patience forgive
Each bullet and each thrust
That we send out!
Lead us not into temptation
That by our wrath Your Divine trial
Terminate too soon!
Us and our nation's friend
Deliver from our hellish foe
And his servants on earth!
Yours is the kingdom, Germany's land
To us through Your armored Hand
Must come glory and strength.[5]

The belligerent derives his convictions, as this example shows, from the image he has constructed of the enemy. Belligerence lives off a clear enemy image. The opponent is portrayed as the devil's servant, the instrument of a hellish power, the incarnation of evil. To oppose such a foe, war—especially in the name of God—is justified. To oppose him one may mount a crusade.

Belligerence prevails first and foremost among people who think they can distinguish clearly between good and evil, black and white. They tend to find the good only in themselves, and evil only in others. Many of them are convinced that they themselves have experienced a personal conversion and have turned away from evil toward the good. They often claim that only those who have had that kind of personal turnaround can take part in the peace of God. The affirmation of God's peace then becomes the exclusive possession of the converted.

The sincerity of conversion, however, must be demonstrated in the lasting and unbreakable loyalty with which the converted cling to specific declarations held to be at the core of biblical teaching. The emphasis on personal conversion, and a fixation on a few doctrinal statements held to be totally inviolable, are prominent marks of a religious fundamentalism.

Because this fundamentalism is confronted with the clear opposition of believers and nonbelievers, of good people and bad people, political belligerents and religious fundamentalists frequently unite into an inseparable entity. Since the enemy stands outside the peace of God, the use of military force against that enemy is justified.

Besides a clear enemy image and an exclusive understanding of God's peace, this way of thinking is marked by one more trait: while its representatives tend to consider violence an appropriate means to use in international conflicts, they also affirm merciless severity and punishing force as appropriate measures to be used by the state against its own citizens and by parents against their children. The state's punishing force and parents' disciplinary force are not considered exceptions that should be used only as a last resort when all other means have failed, but rather they are deemed to be the rule.

Human beings, so goes the conviction behind this view, learn only when forced to: "Who does not want to hear must feel." Social psychologists call this attitudinal syndrome an "authoritarian-punitive complex." It greatly intensifies and stabilizes a political bent toward war.

Realism

More widespread than belligerence is the attitude I call "realism." Its starting point is the commitment of all mankind, but especially of Christians, to peace. But this commitment to peace, it is added, must be carried out under the conditions of a world not yet liberated. It is characteristic of realists that for them evil is not yet conquered but is instead still at work. That is why peace breakers appear again and again.

Peace is not a secure possession but is instead repeatedly endangered. It must be protected or reestablished. As means to protect and to reestablish peace, however, threats and the use of force cannot be excluded in principle. Instead, one must note that violence is the possibility of last resort.

This stance is the starting point of the just war doctrine I have already described, which was introduced into Christian thinking by Augustine in the fifth century. Medieval theologians took it up and expanded it. The sixteenth-century reformers—Luther, Calvin, Zwingli, and their colleagues—also endorsed it.

Let us remember the doctrine's decisive starting point: if in the most extreme need—*ultima ratio*—war measures have to be undertaken to restore peace, clear criteria must be followed. Every one must be able to test out whether the situation warrants morally justifiable participation in war. These criteria were developed by ancient philosophy, refined by Christian theologies, and adopted by modern civil law. When the reformers adopted the medieval notion of a just war, they made the intention of the doctrine more obvious by adding two clarifying points.

(1) A war started for reasons of faith and religion can never be a just war, for faith does not permit itself to be spread or defended by violent means. Faith is dependent solely and exclusively on the power of the Word and on acts of love.

(2) According to the reformers, the only just war is a defensive one, and every attack is precluded. No one played with the idea of a preventive defensive war. But modern civil law expanded the criteria by adopting a criterion to protect civilian populations and thus demanded the differentiation of combatants from noncombatants.

These clarifying points could not, however, prevent the just war doctrine from being turned into a cheap instrument to justify every war. The main requirement was that the war be declared by a government authority, and everything followed from that. That is why one talked of the wars between nations as "two-sided just war." Every nation claimed God for its own cause, "God is with us," just as they claimed justice for their side. By this time the original intention of the just war doctrine had disappeared completely.

Nor did the triumphal march of modern war technology start as late as the development of the atomic weapons. Modern war really started with the increase by leaps and bounds of the weapons' destructive power by the end of the nineteenth century. Since that time no war can be considered a just war in the sense of the doctrine.

In the face of the destructive means available, the threat and the use of violence will never be able to obey the commandment regarding the appropriateness of the means. Modern air wars are excellent examples for the waging of a war that certainly no longer distinguishes military persons from the civilian population. It is valid to say that not just since the first atom bombs were dropped on Hiroshima and Nagasaki in August 1945, but rather, since the First World War, all warfare has proven to be unjust when judged by the criteria of the just war doctrine.

And the Gulf War is no exception. If the claim was made that it was a just war anyway, this shows only that the doctrine has changed its function. It is no longer used to test a government's waging of war and to refuse to support that war if necessary. It serves instead solely to justify the military use of force.

Yet some people question whether the just war doctrine, when compared to other options, does not have the great advantage of being closer to reality. They declare that the doctrine factors in the evil of humankind and confronts the fact that there will always be people who break the peace. That is precisely the reason why the criteria of the just war doctrine are applied repeatedly even though their assumptions no longer hold.

No matter how seriously one must take this argument, one must nevertheless add that the realism of this doctrine tempts people to view the present reality ideologically. The adherents of the just war doctrine refuse to admit that, in face of the horrible effect of modern wars, the institution of organized mass killing must itself be rendered obsolete. Those who are convinced that there are such things as just wars see no reason to put an end to the institution of war, no matter how much the destructive power of modern weapons has grown, but that is exactly what the gruesome scale of violence loosed by twentieth-century humanity requires.

Principled Pacifism

This kind of thinking drove out Christian thinking on just war. The concept of "pacifism" originated at exactly the time that people began to be frightened by the potential for destruction made available by modern technology. In 1901, "pacifism," a self-designation of members of the peace movement, surfaced for the first time. It was soon used as a curse word and vilification.

Pacifists, according to the meaning of the word, are people who have committed themselves completely to the task of making peace. The word has a direct connection to the blessing of the peacemakers in Jesus' Sermon on the Mount (Matt. 5:9).

From the very beginning, however, two distinct strands developed within the pacifist movement. These strands are also contained in the Protestant churches of Europe, the United States, and elsewhere. I shall make modified use of Max Weber's distinction between the ethics of principle and those of responsibility in order to characterize the two strands.

The first strand I call "principled pacifism." At its core is the conviction that violence is taboo. Its focus is on the conscience of the individual and the resulting consequences. Principled pacifists feel duty-bound by their conscience to renounce every kind of violence. They seek to obey this orientation in their own behavior as well as in their public life. They are linked with the Anabaptists of the sixteenth century who refused to take part in any tasks of government because these were interwoven with the use of force. That is why the primary interest of principled pacifists is not a concern with how coexistence can be peaceful, but rather with how they personally can forgo all forms of violence.

The representatives of this attitude are often prepared to suffer heavy burdens if that is required by their conviction. They do not recoil before suffering and persecution. They counter the state's use of violence with convincing signs of personal acts of love and helpfulness. Moving examples of this are found in the history of the Quakers, Mennonites, and other peace churches.

It is this demeanor of unconditional and unequivocal nonviolence that over the course of a long time provided the legal interpretation of conscientious objection in Germany. The law providing for the right to refuse to carry arms for reason of conscience was intended to be limited to the principled pacifists, who were referred to as "pacifists in principle."

Responsible Pacifists

As convincing and moving as the inherent humaneness of a consistent principled pacifist is, the limitations of this position are nevertheless manifested in the question of how, in a world inundated with weapons, peace can possibly be secured, and what its form should be once secured. This question drove many people away from pure principled pacifism.

People tried to make the impulse toward nonviolence bear fruit as steps that could be undertaken to stem the violence actually present. I call their stance "responsible pacifism." It has sometimes also been called "organizational pacifism." At its core is taking up the task of preventing the outbreak of violence and ending the use of violence. Its focus is on the means that can succeed in resolving the conflicts which keep erupting between peoples, utilizing politics instead of military force. Responsible pacifists start with solidarity with victims of violence. Their intention is to prevent human beings from being continually delivered up to the violence of war.

Responsible pacifism insists on subduing violence through the law. Its model is the creation of European territorial states during the transition from the Middle Ages to modern times. During this transition it was of decisive importance that conflicts within the individual states no longer be decided by means of violent self-help on grounds of feudal rights. Instead, the states were given a monopoly on the use of force and the means of judicial decisions.

According to the responsible pacifists, the European Union needs a parallel to this transition from feudal law to state monopoly on the use of force. This parallel can succeed only if, in the community of nations, those organs that have the means and the authority to resolve conflicts are acknowledged. Toward the end of the eighteenth century, Immanuel Kant, in his proposal "Towards Eternal Peace," sketched this kind of organ when he posited a federation of republics.

Kant's plan was taken up in the twentieth century with the founding of the League of Nations and the United Nations. Yet up to now the United Nations has been denied the freedom to act in necessary ways if it really is to function as an international peace authority. Even responsible pacifists have to concede that there is still a wide chasm between hope and reality. This wide chasm was demonstrated in the Gulf War.

Christian decision making regarding the issue of war and peace was, for a long time, shaped above all by the mutually exclusive positions of realism and principled pacifism. And even today some Christian groups advocate the belligerent position as well. But Christian leaning toward responsible pacifism is becoming more and more apparent. In an age when nuclear mass destruction is possible, many streams that earlier flowed side-by-side without touching now are converging. Of course there remains an unbridgeable difference in style between the convictions of responsible pacifists and the attitudes of belligerents who still see in war a means of carrying out the fight between good and evil.

But in the course of time Christian ethics, having undergone difficult periods of confusion, has more and more clearly put the mission to secure peace by political rather than warlike means in the forefront. It was not just historical factors like the two World Wars of our century and the modern weapons of mass destruction that have furthered this lesson. There are also elements in the Christian faith itself that can be stated in the words of the Ecumenical Convention in Dresden in 1989:

Christians let themselves be led by the principal missions

- to procure justice for the neglected and oppressed;
- to serve peace with nonviolent means;
- to protect and promote life on earth.[6]

THE GULF WAR AND RELIGION'S LOSS OF CREDIBILITY

If we now take one more look back on the Gulf War, an ominous correlation between religion and war becomes apparent. The role of religion was disastrous for the war, for it was turned into a weapon by both sides, "God with us." In America, of all places, where the Constitution clearly separates church and state, the president made effective use of public prayer. This was, in a sense, as offensive as the way Saddam Hussein shed his secular socialist feathers to emerge a Muslim fundamentalist.

Religion stepped forward primarily in its belligerent form, and sometimes in its realistic one. Public opinion often disparaged opponents of the war as principled ethicists or principled pacifists. The responsible pacifist stand was pushed into the background in this kind of thinking about war and peace.

The war was disastrous for religion. It gave fundamentalism added impetus in the Islamic states. And it lent Europeans and American an apparently clear conscience when talking about the "Arabs" with a feeling of cultural superiority. They quickly forgot that the objections to Western models of progress had occurred precisely in Islamic fundamentalism. Shortcomings in our own culture were now easily ignored or suppressed.

Like the Soviet empire's collapse, the Gulf War apparently immunized the image of our civilization against criticism. The war served as a welcome frame for a new enemy image. Within a few weeks the talk of "Arabs" supplanted "Communists" in the conversations at the neighborhood tavern, and not just there. Under the stimulus of the Gulf War, we quickly regained an enemy image, a phenomenon that had grown dear to us.

Interest in Islam grew in many places because of the war. The number of people who wanted to learn about the basic beliefs of the Muslim faith increased. Yet this did not help the religion gain in credibility. Instead, the information was sought in a way to intensify its strangeness. There was increasing doubt whether any religion, so easily adapted to fit political interests, could lay claim to any independent truth of its own.

The observation that both sides used religion to support them in the Gulf War contributed quite a bit to the growing indifference to religion. Religions that enlist participation in the service of the ruling interests lose their credibility—and that verdict applies to Christianity just as much as to Islam. The Gulf War has played a large part in the drive toward secularism that we are presently witnessing, a fact not yet sufficiently understood.

CHAPTER FIVE

Military Violence after the Cold War

The Gulf War must be remembered above all for the victims it created. It should also be remembered because it was interpreted as heralding a new world order, a contribution to a new political order both necessary and possible after the Cold War. The quotation from President George Bush's speech of January 17, 1991, at the beginning of "Desert Storm" is appropriate to this point:

> I hope that this fight will not last long, and that the casualties will be held to an absolute minimum. This is a historical moment. We made great progress this past year to end the long era of conflict and cold war. Ahead of us is the chance for us and for future generations to form a new world order, a world in which the rule of law and not the rule of the jungle will guide the behavior of the nations. If we are successful, and we will be, we have a real chance for a new world order in which a trustworthy United Nations can assume its peacemaking role in order to fulfill the promise and vision of its founders.

And on January 31, 1991, Bush told the members of both houses of Congress:

> There is more at stake than a small country. It is a grand idea: a new world order in which different nations join together for a common cause, to realize the universal hope of humanity for peace and security, liberty and the rule of law.

Sentences like these align the Gulf War into the series of challenges facing the community of nations after the Cold War. The four decades of conflict between East and West were marked, among other things, by a balance of intimidation intended to prevent a "hot war." These efforts did not prevent regional wars, but—in spite of discord—they did prevent a worldwide military apocalypse.

After the collapse of the Soviet Union and the dissolution of the Warsaw Pact, the struggle for dominance between the United States and the Union of Soviet Socialist Republics is just as much part of the past as is the system of nations opposing nations on the European continent. As a result, fear of a great atomic war has also abated.

And yet peace is no more certain now. Instead, a disquieting destabilization is taking place in regions in which the great powers were once interested in maintaining stability. Ethnic/ national conflicts that had remained hidden during the cold war are now erupting with volcanic force. States that were formerly forced into unity are crumbling.

These new conflicts are neither national wars nor civil wars in the old style. They take place in a realm between those two types of war. Their very new style is one reason why governments and international organizations are at a loss as to how to react to them. The hatred fomented between peoples who coexisted for decades under the same political system is extremely shocking to outsiders.

The states that once made up Yugoslavia are sunk in war and terrorism, and ceasefires and peace enforcement by the United States remain tenuous. In several successor states to the Soviet Union, such as in Chechneya, there is an ominous disquiet. In Somalia, which the United States formerly protected and supplied with arms because of its strategic position at the horn of Africa, adherents of inimical clans are mangling each other with these same weapons to such an extent that the whole country is reduced to a prenational condition. Similar things are beginning to happen in other regions of the earth. The question of how to safeguard security and support peace is assuming new urgency.

The end of the East/West conflict not only brought opportunities for a new arrangement of peace, but also brought new risks. Whether or not the community of nations can take advantage of these changed circumstances to build a new peace arrangement is an open question.

George Bush responded to these altered circumstances in 1991 with a decisive program. Attributing to the Gulf War a key importance for the "new world order," he stressed that this world arrangement was to be based on peace and security, freedom and the rule of law. But tying the Gulf War to the project of a new world order has much wider and weightier implications, primarily:

(1) The new world order starts with the primacy of the rich industrial states, and therefore reinforces the colonial (or rather, the neo-colonial) structures of dependence between North and South.

(2) The new world order has to be supported by military force; securing the supply of raw materials to the industrial nations, such as oil, is sufficient motive for intervening militarily.

(3) If a regional conflict touches on the economic interests of the Western industrial nations, it provides the United States with a reason to assume the role of being the world's police force.

(4) Wars waged with modern technology of destruction are "just wars" too.

The "new world order" proclaimed by Bush did not start with the idea that the institution of war must be overcome. Nor was Bush prepared to forgo the means of war and to renounce war by making great political efforts, even in the face of the terrible weapons of destruction. Instead, Bush reverted to the by-now conventional notion of the Prussian general Von Clausewitz, who suggested that war is "a continuation of political traffic with the interjection of other means."[1]

Thinking like that resonated in Germany as well. Even while the war lasted, the numbers grew—among intellectuals as well as in the churches—of people who were again convinced of the inevitability of warlike violence and thus rejected the protest against the war on the grounds that protest was unrealistic and irresponsible principled pacifism. They called for a new form of realism that would deal with the necessity of war.

The subject under discussion since this new turn to "realism" is the issue of national military units serving outside their normally fixed sphere of activity, such as the U.S. presence in Bosnia in 1996. What is demanded is not only their participation in United Nations peacekeeping missions but also in UN combat missions or NATO interventions out of the area. With the end of the Cold War the issue of military force is once again open to debate.

ETHICAL PRINCIPLES OF PEACE

A human being's responsibility extends to the limit of his or her power. Political communities are no different. Their responsibility is determined by the extent of their economic, military, and political power. The political responsibility of the United States therefore stretches as far as the effects of the power at its disposal are manifest—particularly its economic strength and its role in world trade. With this power it shares in the expansion of the European/North American industrial civilization and its ambivalent effects.

No one can ignore the fact that Western science and trade have altered the living conditions of the world as a whole. Therefore the responsibility we share today takes on a global dimension, encompassing the living space of the whole planet earth. No one who seeks to protect nature, to live in a society honoring human dignity, and to have peace among nations can evade this dimension. The new debate regarding the mission of the armed forces, the role of NATO, and the future form of the United Nations must also be seen in this context.

The collapse of the Central and East European one-party dictatorships has radically altered the old political order. This applies to Germany in particular, since with unification it has gained as many unexpected and unresolved problems as it has gained in influence. Located at the seamline of the once split and suddenly unified continent, Germany has a particular obligation to make sure that a political system is established in Europe that can be labeled as an arrangement of peace.

The ethic of peace has no finished concepts at its disposal to cope with the new situation. It, too, must first digest the historical upheavals we have witnessed since the second half of the 1980s. All peace-ethical efforts before 1989 were conducted in the context of the East/West conflict and its system of deterrence.

True, research on peace and peace-ethics had already been underway for a long time, searching for a concept of peace that meant more than mere absence of war and warlike violence. Yet, intensified by the arms race of the late 1970s and early 1980s, these were primarily criticisms of nuclear deterrence, rejections of means of mass destruction of all kinds, declarations of readiness to renounce arms, or pleas to find means of preserving mutual security.

Discussions on peace in the early 1980s concentrated on the problem of the East/West conflict, as the peace-ethical stance of the "conciliatory process" aptly demonstrates. Although this stance was and is dedicated to the three goals of justice, peace, and protection of creation, nevertheless, peace is, for the most part, understood as the absence of military force in achieving these three goals.

We embark on virgin territory when we talk of peace-ethics, and cannot claim to possess adequate answers to the new questions already. But these discussions on the ethics of peace did lead to some insights that transcend the East/West conflict and should therefore be preserved and noted within our new circumstances. I note four enduring insights that were either arrived at or strengthened in these discussions:

(1) Justice, avoidance of violence, and preservation of nature are basic elements of peace, belong together, and must not be

played one against the other. The most important options to achieve justice for the poor, to free persons from violence, and to preserve nature, must together be developed for today's required strategies for peace.

(2) In dealing with political conflicts, the nonmilitary instruments to end those conflicts must first be elaborated and strengthened. We reverse our priorities when we expand our military instruments to protect and reestablish peace. Even when the doctrine of "just war" can no longer be preserved in the form it has had heretofore, one decisive criterion of that dogma must not be forgotten: the use of military force must never be seen as *more* than a means of last resort (*ultima ratio*).

(3) The most dangerous aspect of military means is that those means are linked to the logic of exclusiveness, which declares that peace can only be established *against* the other, not *with* the other. This is often linked to the search for an enemy. An enemy must be found against whom armed force must be used to protect the peace. One of the important and lasting insights of our discussions on peace-ethics and peace-policies is to reject this logic of exclusivity and the search for enemies. When new political conflicts are once again interpreted in categories of blocs and in foe-images, it violates these insights—and this violation occurred more than enough in the Gulf War.

(4) Peace can only be established on the basis of relationships of mutual respect and the exercise of common or collective security. Mutual respect does not exclude, but rather includes, criticizing an undemocratic regime's practices that violate human rights. But mutual respect *does* exclude using human rights solely as an excuse to criticize others. And mutual respect encourages using such nonmilitary interventions as will create conditions that further human rights and thereby also further mutual respect.

The exercise of common or collective security requires strengthening transnational institutions whose legitimate mission is the prevention and suppression of military conflicts.

In many groups, these insights are represented more often by *responsible* pacifists than by *principled* pacifists. Responsible pacifism's more obvious contouring is seen in the important results of the struggle regarding nuclear deterrence. This struggle demonstrated that it is not enough to merely oppose the use of military force. What matters is preventing it effectively. Being aware that one rejects the use of military violence—in spite of the fact that it is nevertheless being used—cannot soothe one's conscience. Preventing and suppressing violence require more than merely being convinced that one is personally committed to nonviolence.

Murderous violence in new and terrifying forms has broken out not only in the destroyed Yugoslavia since the Cold War, but in other parts of the world as well. It is our political responsibility to deal with the means to end such violence.

PEACEKEEPING DUTIES OF THE COMMUNITY OF NATIONS

In the preamble to its Constitution, the Federal Republic of Germany pledges, "as equal member of a united Europe, to serve the peace of the world." This constitutional orientation to peace shapes its friendly attitude toward international law and its openness to eliminating war by participating in a system of collective security.

The hope that such a system of collective security will be instituted is directed primarily at the United Nations. The goal written in the UN charter is "to protect future generations against the scourge of war which has twice in our lifetime brought untold suffering on mankind." To maintain world peace and international security, and to make sure that "military weapons will be used only in the common interest in future" are among the primary duties of the UN. It is committed to:

> take effective collective measures to prevent and to eliminate threats to peace, to suppress aggressive actions and other peace-breaking acts, and to settle and resolve international conflicts or situations leading to breaking the peace by peaceful means in accordance with the principles of fairness and international law.[2]

The actualization of these goals, however, can occur only when the United Nations is granted the necessary instruments to institute a worldwide effective monopoly on intervention. This suggestion should not be equated with a notion of a world state or world government. Rather, it is based on the assumption that the states have entrusted a specific mission—namely, the prevention and termination of violent aggression in international disagreements—to a transnational authority.

Hopes for just that have existed since the beginnings of the United Nations, and the dramatic upheaval in international relations begun in the 1980s may advance these hopes. True, actualization must include reform in the United Nations. The dominance of the five veto powers in the Security Council in particular—the United States, Russia, China, Great Britain, and France—must be replaced by a "democratic" decision process.

Even after the Cold War, the primacy of using nonmilitary means rather than military means to enforce peace policies must not be abandoned. Now as before the extent and horror of modern weapons of destruction force the international community to commit themselves to use political methods to overcome the institution of war.

Participating in a system of collective security makes no sense at all if the purpose is to make war "possible to wage" again, thus making war a "normal" instrument of policy. Instead, the purpose should be to contribute toward eliminating war. That is why peace policies as well as policies for the future aimed at resolving the causes of conflict must maintain primacy over military security policies.

And that is also the decisive starting point for a discussion about future tasks and structures of the United Nations. Confining oneself to the issues of peacekeeping missions and combat troops is not enough. One must instead start with the insight that the United Nations occupies a key position for preserving peace and for resolving the causes of conflict in future policies. Its continuing functions of maintaining security policies enforced by the military are to be included in this framework.

These goals are not attainable without a structural alteration in the United Nations. The Stockholm Initiative for Global Security and World Order presented convincing proposals for such an alteration in May 1991.[3] These proposals were supported by Jimmy Carter, Benazir Bhutto, Eduard Shevardnadze, Vaclav Havel, Julius Nyerere, and Edward Heath, among others.

The proposals included strengthening UN jurisdictions and authority to act, establishing regional conferences for security and cooperation, giving priority to nonmilitary conflict resolutions (including economic sanctions), limiting arms deals and disarmament in developing countries, initiating peace dividends of structural changes in developing countries, organizing peacekeeping and peace-initiating measures supported by the military if necessary—through the UN—and thus developing a monopoly on intervention in the hands of the United Nations.

We still have a long way to go before these proposals become reality. Secretary General Boutros Boutros-Ghali presented his "Agenda for Peace" in the summer of 1992, which developed a clear and convincing structure for the missions of the peace policy with which the UN must deal. This "Agenda for Peace," to be elaborated by an "Agenda for Development" at a later date, distinguished four basic areas of action in securing peace:

- *Conflict prophylaxis,* especially through preventive diplomacy;
- *Peacemaking,* intervening in a military conflict until a truce or peace treaty has been achieved;
- *Peacekeeping,* by enforcing truce or peace treaty conditions and by protecting humanitarian actions;
- And finally, post-conflict *peace-building.*

Certainly this division is not without problems. Above all, in many situations that require a robust military presence to keep the peace and enforce earlier peacekeeping missions, it is not easy to draw the line in peacemaking. And the line between preventive diplomacy and peacekeeping is relativized by using preventive peacekeeping in some cases. We must nevertheless hold on to these distinctions, for the issue is whether the United Nations can intervene directly in a war and thus use direct military force against the warring parties in some situations, or whether it is limited to securing a truce or conditions for peace and may resort to armed force only in cases of self-defense or in police action.

The distinction between the tasks of peacekeeping and peacemaking is just as necessary as the distinction between peacekeeping missions and combat missions. Peacekeepers serve as election observers, police, political or technical experts, among other duties. Peacemaking, on the other hand, includes—besides diplomatic interventions and economic or political sanctions—combat missions intended to provide peace enforcement by military means.

PEACEKEEPING MISSIONS

Peacekeeping troops were not foreseen in the 1945 Charter of the United Nations, but they are based on the praxis of the Security Council since 1948. The Council institutes an action when it has the agreement of the conflicting parties, and forms an international peacekeeping unit composed of troops from member states. Participation is voluntary, not legally required.

Peacekeepers are not required to achieve direct conflict resolution by combat, but they do have the duty to create the preconditions for negotiating a political resolution by weakening the conflict. Some of their traditional functions are the maintenance and control of a truce, protection of humanitarian missions, and control over a comprehensive peace process.

The participants in peacekeeping operations stress that nonpartisanship, deescalating conflict, and extreme restraint in the use of weapons (minimal force) are their indispensable principles. These principles must be maintained even when the duties of the peacekeepers are expanded to include preventive measures or particularly "robust" missions in regions in crisis.

An impressive example of the diversity of peacekeeping missions is the peace mission in Namibia from 1989 to 1990. The unit took on tasks that far transcended military duties. It took care of calming hostilities, assumed control of the police, supervised the withdrawal of South African troops, and provided for secure free and fair elections. It accelerated the revoking of discriminatory laws, the execution of amnesty for political prisoners and the repatriation of political exiles. The goal of all these measures was to support a political transformation to achieve the self-determination of Namibia with a constitution incorporating human rights.

The peacekeeping troops sent to Namibia included military, civilian, and police personnel. One can count on this kind of combination in future as well. A concept that would expand on that of the peacekeepers is to have member states organize nonmilitary peace corps and put them at the disposal of the United Nations in cases of environmental and famine catastrophes among others.

COMBAT MISSIONS

A seeming paradox exists between peacekeeping missions and combat missions. Although peacekeeping missions are not mentioned in the United Nations Charter, they have been carried out in practice. Combat missions, on the other hand, were provided for in the Charter but have never been actually carried out in accord with the UN rules.

Chapters VI and VII of the Charter describe the types of action the Security Council can take in the case of conflicts, and also describe the possible peacemaking actions. Chapter VI deals with the peaceful resolution of conflicts and also describes the Security Council's investigative rights, and its possibilities for action—one of which, appeal to the International Court, is a very important one—and develops practical proposals for mediation.

Chapter VII deals with measures against threatened or actual breaking of the peace and aggressive actions. In the foreground of measures open to the Security Council are peaceful sanctions. Among these, specific mention is made of total or partial interruptions in trade, traffic in goods and people, and communications, as well as breaking off diplomatic relations.

Only secondarily are military sanctions discussed. The Security Council can:

> with air, sea, or land combat troops carry out measures necessary to preserve or reestablish world peace and international security. These can include demonstrations, blockades, or other air, sea, or land combat troop actions from members of the United Nations.[4]

The Security Council must make separate agreements with each member state beforehand for the contribution of combat troops by these states.[5] Those member states that are obligated to take part in specific military sanctions but are not members of the Security Council must be included in the Council's deliberations on the pertinent issue. Plans for executing military sanctions are set by the Security Council in common with a specially appointed military High Command committee.[6] The actions to be undertaken are communicated to the participating members.

The regulation expresses the attempt to create a United Nations intervention authority while at the same time respecting the sovereignty of the participating states. This is also manifest in that the chapter on UN measures in cases of threatened or actual breaking of the peace closes with an article reenforcing the right of self-defense of member states in the sense of a right to collective defense.[7]

Because of this discordance, up to now there have been no UN military sanctions in accordance with the rules of the Charter. No special agreements have as yet been made with any member state with regard to contributing combat troops. The Military High Command Committee has not yet fulfilled any effective function in cases of conflict. The separation between planning and execution of sanctions has proven to be impractical.

Until now military measures by individual member states who could appeal to Security Council resolutions have taken place, but no military sanctions by the Security Council itself have been carried out. Even when Chapter VII in general was referred to, the mechanisms described therein were never actualized.

"Desert Storm" against Iraq in 1991 was not a military sanction in accord with the rules of Chapter VII of the UN Charter. The same applies to the measures prohibiting flights over Bosnia. Authorization by member states to conduct military missions should not be confused with military actions by the Security Council itself.

Therefore, what must be remembered is that so far there has never been a case of a United Nations military mission to reestablish peace in accordance with the provisions set forth in the UN Charter. For the time being the UN lacks the required instrument. Experience so far has shown that this kind of combat mission can only be carried out in the sense of the UN charter if the UN would also be given supreme command of the troops contributed by the member states. And up to now the United States in particular has not been prepared to cede command. Whether this can change during Clinton's administration cannot yet be assessed.

And yet agreement to participate in UN combat missions would make sense only under those conditions. Moreover, the composition and working methods of the Security Council would have to be altered in such a way that developing nations have a chance to participate. Under present conditions, in any case, it is false for any country to aver that participation in UN combat missions is required by virtue of membership in the UN.

THE BALKAN WAR AND MILITARY INTERVENTION

There is cause to fear that empowering a country to participate in UN combat missions could be used to legitimize measures that in no way are executed within the framework of the UN but rather in that of NATO, the European Union (EEC), or ad hoc military alliances. Have not the horrors of the Balkan conflicts over secession, has not the utter contempt for basic human rights, victimizing Bosnian women in particular, amply demonstrated that in some situations only the willingness to intervene militarily can rescue human life and dignity and put an end to military terrorism?

No politically responsible person planned direct military intervention. The West European states had decided against it. Possibly the economic interests involved did not seem so urgent that it would pay to intervene militarily. But above all, no one had any idea how external intervention could overcome the hatred and disunity between the warring parties.

True, a military intervention in the Balkans on the model of the Gulf War would certainly lead to a short interruption in the combat, but the causes of the conflict and the smoldering fire of spreading nationalism would not be eliminated. One could not create peace for the "ethnic patchwork quilt" of Bosnia. Added conflicts—in the province of Kosova with an Albanian population of more than 90 percent, in the Serbian province of Vojvodina with a non-Serbian population of 50 percent, or for Macedonia, which will perhaps make territorial claims on Greece and Bulgaria—would not be avoided but would perhaps even be intensified.

The partisan resistance of World War II in Yugoslavia still enjoys a legendary reputation, and the geographic conditions favor that kind of warfare. That is why the notion that massive military intervention can permanently stop acts of violence is especially mistaken. This example demonstrates that military force cannot solve political problems but can, in the most favorable cases, merely prepare a solution or make a solution easier to achieve.

The less trust there is in the chances of a military solution in the Balkan states, the more regrettable it is that until the United States sent peacekeeping troops in late 1995, no other policies were instituted with the necessary consistency. The European states failed for too long to reach a unanimous and clear position with regard to the Balkan conflict. The trade and weapons embargo against Serbia was imposed much too late and much too half-heartedly enforced. One of the depressing patterns in public discussion is that some commentators accept as a given the alleged impossibility of succeeding with economic sanctions and so want to justify the inevitability of military intervention.

So what remains is the depressing insight that any possible establishment of peace coming solely from the outside is extremely limited in a conflict such as the one in the Balkans. Yet this insight brings with it the obligation to use those remaining possibilities with more decisiveness than has yet been done. These possibilities are primarily in three areas:

First is direct humanitarian assistance to the victims of the war's terrorism. Food transports into the areas threatened by hunger, providing medicines and medical supplies, and sheltering the victims of rape are prominent examples. On the one hand these are carried out by governments, but on the other hand a lot of assistance comes from nongovernmental organizations and volunteer groups—including various women's groups and doctors' groups, such as the International Red Cross.

Second, governments and volunteer groups must contribute to efforts to tear down the hatred between the various ethnic populations—in many cases a hatred of long standing, in others a hatred willfully provoked—and to develop new opportunities for understanding. Just how decisive reconciliation efforts and the building of trust are in preparing a lasting peace can be seen in the example of the opposite conditions in the former Yugoslavia. Humanitarian actions are an important starting point for this kind of reconciling service.

Third, the religious communities that have allowed themselves to slide disastrously into taking sides in the Balkan conflict must free themselves from this functionalism and contribute their share to understanding and peace.

To peace itself there is no other way than the way of political solutions. Even if the solutions proposed for Bosnia by Cyrus Vance and David Owen were very ambivalent because they come much too close to the notions of "ethnic purity" of a territory, there is no alternative to the search for negotiated solutions. Flight bans or other military sanctions, economic boycotts, or political interventions can all serve to bring the hostile parties to the negotiating table and move them toward a bearable peace agreement. One hopes that the Dayton peace agreements of 1995 will foster a permanent solution.

SUMMARY

If the United Nations is to develop a combat troop under its own command, international military interventions must remain extremely limited. Every urge to intervene is disastrous, as was shown in the Gulf War. History has shown that we must cling to the *culture of restraint* and must prove our commitment to peace by giving consistent priority to nonmilitary measures and by participating in peacekeeping missions.

The course of Balkan conflict does not justify giving up the principle that we must maintain solidarity with its victims. This must be manifested in decisive humanitarian assistance, practical reconciliation efforts, and effective contributions to the political solution to the causes of the conflict.

Notions of expanding the independent mission of the armed forces beyond defense duties and equal notions of participating in independent NATO missions out of the area are in no way covered by peace-ethical considerations. The planetary responsibility of the 1990s does not contain any new independent duties for the United States army, German armed forces, NATO, or the European Union. Instead, the greater obligation is to strengthen and expand the UN's peace function.

CHAPTER SIX

Violence against Humanity and Nature

The Necessity for a Planetary Ethos

We are standing at a turning point in our ethical orientation. Behind us is a time during which the possibilities of individual lifestyles proliferated, and the norms applicable to everyone were almost shredded in the process. In the meantime, many people have discovered that this proliferation has led to a dead-end. Our most pressing question is, What still binds all of us together? The time of limitless growth that seemed to make everything one could think of possible is gone. Once again the question is being raised, What is essential to life?

Such a turning point veils great perils. One of the greatest dangers is that defenders of simple answers and simple slogans like "law and order" or national pride are once again offering them as guiding stars.

In a world that has coalesced into one world, whoever offers an escape into simple solutions does not serve new orientation but rather endangers freedom. Great efforts will be required to prevent the search for new binding forces from falling back into old dependencies. Those who want to avoid that must start to search for a form of coexistence that not only is in agreement with the freedom of every individual but that also helps to unfold their freedom.

The new binding forces being sought must not strangle freedom. They should oppose wilfulness and arbitrariness, and counteract uninhibited egotism, but they should leave room for diversity in lifestyles. Today, too, the rules meriting respect are those that help people coexist in their diversity, free of fear and free from want.

This task is not a new one. The basic text of Jewish and Christian ethics—the Decalogue or Ten Commandments—already served freedom, sharpening the rules without which a life in freedom would not succeed. From the Ten Commandments we learn that, if viewed correctly, there is no contradiction between freedom and binding force, between plurality and common life. Rather, the greater the variety in ethical orientations existing not only among the cultures and religious orientations but also within individual societies, the more urgent is the question whether there are binding minimum standards of behavior that must not be dissolved into pluralistic arbitrariness. And, vice versa, only when a core of commonly acknowledged principles is found and adhered to can the diversity of cultural, religious, and ethical orientations unfold in freedom.

I have used a great many examples in the preceding chapters to show that it is precisely multicultural and multireligious societies which need an understanding about the principles necessary to enable the coexistence of many different people. I combined that insight with the thesis that acknowledgment of equal dignity for all human beings and thus respect for elementary human rights are inviolable principles of coexistence. Now I will attempt to explain the key concepts of human dignity and human rights, and then ask what new ethical tasks lie ahead of us.

HUMAN DIGNITY IN ANTIQUITY AND IN THE CHRISTIAN TRADITION

Ideas of human dignity and human rights have been shaped by a long historical development. Thus, the sense of these ideas is best explained by way of a short historical summary.

Talk of human dignity has appeared in two distinct forms in European tradition. The first refers to the specific rank of particular persons within a society; the concept of dignity (*dignitas*) is here related to that of honor (*honor*). The second refers to that which distinguishes humanity from all other forms of life and gives a reason for its special position in the cosmos. In the former, the result is different rankings among people; in the latter, the result is the fundamental equality of all humans.

It is true that Greek and Roman philosophies used both forms. But in pre-Christian antiquity primacy was alloted to the thought that dignity was the reason for the authority given to some people to lift them above the rest. In the Christian tradition, on the other hand, the conviction that all human beings possess equal dignity gained the upper hand from the very beginning, stressing the equality of God's children.

That is the revolutionary significance of Christian tradition, joined to Jewish tradition at this point. Both make obvious that the dignity of human beings is taken seriously only by those who respect the God-given equality of human beings. Differences in official positions or duties, of talent or wealth, of gender or nationality, assume only secondary importance in comparison.

This clear statement comes from the biblical creation story, which says that human beings were created in the image of God and so are creatures according to the likeness of God (Gen. 1:26–27). The likeness to God is what distinguishes humans from all other parts of creation, and is the basis for their special dignity. In the New Testament, Paul links up with creation when he states that differences between human beings have no significance when compared to their common existence as children of God.

> As many of you as were baptized into Christ have clothed yourselves with Christ. There is no longer Jew or Greek, there is no longer slave or free, there is no longer male and female; for all of you are one in Christ Jesus.
>
> (Gal. 3:27–28)

The dignity common to all human beings was already ignored at the time of the early church, and even more so in the Middle Ages by both ecclesiastical authorities and the state. It was pushed into the background by three factors: (1) the church teaching on sin; (2) discrimination against certain human groups; and (3) a hierarchical image of society.

First, the concept of the equal dignity of all humans was restricted by the church's understanding of sin. The doctrine of original sin claimed that all humans are from birth subject to the power of evil. It presented a picture of humans who have through sin forfeited all rights before God, and therefore have no control over a dignity that had been withdrawn from all secular and ecclesiastical authorities. The doctrine thus inhibited the development of an independent Christian conception of human dignity and rights.

Second, the equality of human creation was suppressed when Christians differentiated themselves from heretics and non-Christians (Jews and pagans). Until modern times, human dignity was largely considered the privilege of Christians. The declaration that heretics, Jews, and pagans had no right to lay claim to dignity legitimized the terrible methods of the inquisition, pogroms against Jews, and colonialism. Women were excluded from the dignity of all humans in a special manner, as is shown by the persecution of "witches" over the centuries, as well as special cruelty against women heretics, pagans, or Jews.

Third, the Christian notion of human dignity was distorted into an image of society that gave lay people different rankings, as well as a hierarchy in the church. Thus the "bearers of honors" received a higher ranking than the common people with regard to the dignity common to all.

THE NEW TURN TOWARD HUMAN DIGNITY

The idea of the common dignity of all humans based on God's likeness certainly never disappeared entirely. During the age of the Renaissance and Reformation, it ran along three tracks, namely, Italian Renaissance humanism, Spanish late Scholasticism, and the German Reformation.

The Italian humanism of the fifteenth century built upon the concept of humans created in the image of God. For example, the Florentine philosopher Pico della Mirandola, in a famous speech, "About the Dignity of Humans" (published posthumously in 1496), described the human being as a microcosm of God, containing within itself a multitude of choices. He considered a human being's destiny to be one of choosing from among this multitude, and a human's freedom to be contained in the possibility of attaining the highest happiness by his or her own power. Similar thoughts were held by the great Humanists of the sixteenth century, Thomas More and Erasmus of Rotterdam. Thus the Renaissance and humanism prepared the great turnabout in the image of humans.

The modern age, which began with humanism, is characterized by the conviction that human dignity is anchored in the self, namely, in one's rational talents. The more radical thought that humans owed their dignity not to themselves but to their relation to God was often suppressed.

A new challenge to thinking about humans was represented by the European territorial expansions of the fifteenth and sixteenth centuries. Confrontation with the New World after Columbus' voyage in 1492 required some judgment about the strange human beings encountered by the explorers. The most immediate reaction was to place them within the existing distinctions between Christians and pagans, civilized people and barbarians.

Such distinctions led to persistent doubts whether the inhabitants of America could even be recognized as rational beings capable of converting to Christianity. Although the papal bull *Sublimis Deus* of 1537 affirmed formally that the natives should be considered "truly human beings" capable of accepting the Catholic faith and its sacraments, widespread doubts remained about the Indians' rationality and ability to have faith.

A few Spanish theologians, above all Francis of Victoria and Francis Suarez, took an unequivocal position in this controversy. Their starting point was the thesis regarding the sociability of human beings, a controversial point that everyone stumbles on in dealing with the issue of human dignity. In early antiquity, the Roman poet Ovid had already claimed the existence of inexorable enmity between human beings with the terse slogan that man is wolf to man (*homo homini lupus*). Thomas Hobbes, in the middle of the seventeenth century, popularized that slogan in the political thinking of the modern age.

Francis of Victoria countered this view with the declaration that it was the fate of humans to shape a life together with their fellow humans. He expressed it as "man is man to man" (*homo homini homo*). The term *wolf* in this controversy stands for the jealous competition for the scarce means of survival. But the term *human* stands for the capability to have empathy, solidarity, and cooperation.

Regarding the issue of whether the Indians belong to the human race, Francis of Victoria started with the conviction that along with rationality human beings are also given a sense of community and sociability. He concluded that the Indians have a full share of both reason and sociability. Consequently they are owed the same basic rights that every human being can claim. The Spanish conquistadors who had contact with Indians, therefore, not only were forbidden to violate the basic rights of the Indians but were moreover duty-bound to actively defend these rights.

Once again it must be said that what the Spanish and Portuguese masters perpetrated in Latin America totally contradicted the affirmation of the dignity and rights of the native population. Despite that fact, however, the thinking of the late Scholastic theologians was not without sense. Their conception prepared the way for modern international law. They were also advocates of an image of human beings that became the expression of inviolable human rights two hundred years later.

I named the Reformation as a source for the modern concept of human dignity along with Italian humanism and Spanish late Scholasticism. If one seeks the significance of the Lutheran Reformation on this subject, one is directed above all to the central point of reformation theology, namely the doctrine of human justification before God through grace alone. This doctrine—which seems so cumbersome and prudish to us today—expressed in a radical manner not seen since the writings of Paul what makes a human being a human being before God. Neither human achievements nor human circumstances define persons. Instead, human persons are formed by something totally out of human control, namely the gift of divine grace.

In the justification event, humans experience themselves as beings who are not devoted to any specific conditions or definitions of their own, but rather transcend them all. Consequently their dignity cannot be understood as something observable within themselves, for this dignity is promised to them by God's justifying grace. Humans grasp this gift in faith, and only free faith is a true response to grace. Thus faith and freedom belong together. That is why the freedom of faith and with it the freedom of religion constitute the core of human rights.

In Calvin and Calvinism the starting point of human election by God's grace is connected with a particular stress on salvation, thus on the concrete fulfillment of Christian existence—the only purpose of which is to glorify God. The demand for religious freedom and the thought of mutual commitment in the covenant instituted by God are included in this framework. This is the way in which Calvinism prepared for the ethical content of modern human rights. It encouraged forms of expression in church and government that favored human rights.

Yet the manner in which Christian impulses found their way into modern thought was tortuous. Christian impulses were, with many interruptions, secularized in the transition. As much as the early Enlightenment's new concern about dignity and rights of humans owed to Christian roots, so obvious were the disarrangements now taking place with regard to traditional Christian thinking.

One of these shifts was the withdrawing of the doctrine of original sin. The more uninhibited and optimistic the talk was regarding the dignity and abilities of humans, the greater was the need to relativize and secularize the doctrine of original sin. The doctrine appears—in the form of insight into the finiteness and fallibility of humans—merely as a limiting condition of human self realization, no longer a description of the very essence of humans.

Another shift was that human dignity was no longer anchored directly in likeness to God but rather in human rationality. The unity of dignity and reason became a decisive theme in the anthropological turnaround that occurred during the Enlightenment. Now the dignity of all humans was based on the autonomy that is due humans as rational beings. Influential in this anthropological turn is above all the Königsberger philosopher Immanuel Kant, who was the first to dare to offer a definition of human dignity.

According to Kant, dignity is due to those who "are above all price, with no equivalent permitted."[1] What is without equivalent cannot be exchanged for something else and thus is not used up as a means to an end. Means can always be exchanged. Consequently, whatever has dignity must be recognized as an end in itself. The condition for being an end in itself is free self-determination, not conventionality. Insofar as reason is the condition for free self-determination, only rational beings can be viewed as ends in themselves. This leads to the conclusion that only human beings—and, as Kant cautiously assumes, other rational beings such as angels, for example—have dignity.

The reversal in the understanding of humanity, which attained its climax with Kant, places the human person very decidedly in the center of its worldview, and thus bears a strong "anthropocentric" character. It reserves the concept of dignity to the human being as an autonomous subject. It is not content with declaring that, in contrast to other beings, a particular dignity is due human beings who can be recognized by their rational nature. Anthropocentricity claims that dignity can be attributed solely to human beings. As much as it intended to protect human beings from the rule of arbitrariness, so did it at the same time justify the arbitrary rule of humans over nature. Anthropocentricity is unrestrained, since no inherent dignity is attributed to nonhuman nature. The distinction between humanity and nature is precisely the fact that nature can be used as means, humanity cannot.

Only in the face of the ecological crisis was the anthropocentric narrowness of this concept of dignity questioned. Only the destructive consequences of human rule over nature raised the issue of whether nature is due its own dignity, independent of human purposes.

THE TRANSITION TO HUMAN RIGHTS

The recognition of equal dignity of all human beings in the law of individual nations and then in international law is one of the revolutionary events of the modern era. The idea, predating nations, of fundamental rights that the individual can insist on in opposition to the political community was developed in the political conflicts in England in the seventeenth century. In the revolutionary upheavals of the eighteenth century this idea prevailed politically. The modern history regarding liberty is decisively dependent on the connection of human dignity and human rights.

Much weight must be given to the fact that the idea of human rights has entered international law, for this is a history of horrible regressions. The twentieth century has been marked by the experience that protection and support of human rights cannot succeed if left to the national governments alone. Stalin's rule of terror and Nazi Germany's planned program of murder have shown that violations of human rights in *one* nation have direct consequences for the community of nations.

These experiences led to the adoption of human rights in international law, which in turn produced an epoch-making step. The nations were the subject matter of international law from the very beginning; it was unequivocally *inter*national law. With the inclusion of human rights, the individual human person was acknowledged as subject matter for international law. This far-reaching reshaping and expansion of international law is of incisive importance, even though the legal instruments to protect human rights have until the present been only partially developed. One important issue still left unresolved is how far massive human rights violations may justify the intervention—perhaps military—of the community of nations, and who is permitted to function as initiator of this intervention. The apartheid policy in South Africa, the disagreements in the Near East, and the war of terror in the Balkans are three different situations where this issue has been raised emphatically. No convincing answer has yet been found. Nevertheless it is obvious that the traditional national state will alter its function and its form to the extent that the legal instruments to protect human rights in international law are improved.

Being included in international law is also of epochal importance to the concept of human rights. It now makes sense to differentiate between human rights in a broad sense, civil rights, basic rights, and finally human rights in a narrow sense.

Human rights in a broad sense are those rights due to all human beings irrespective of their skin color, nationality, political or religious convictions, social status or economic influence, gender, or age. These human rights are concentrated around the freedom and equality of human persons as well as the share they possess in social goods and political decisions. These are not rights granted by the state but rather predate states. They are inviolable and inalienable.

The state may neither deny nor revoke these rights, nor can any individual renounce them, either voluntarily or under pressure. To limit specific human rights is thus legitimate only when this is absolutely necessary for the sake of maintaining other equally important rights. Individual persons are always the bearers of human rights, therefore it is always a matter of individual rights, not collective rights.

Civil rights are those rights that do not apply to all humans as humans but rather solely to citizens of a state. Examples of civil rights, according to the Bonn constitution, are freedom of assembly, freedom to organize, and freedom to choose careers. One example of a human right not tied to citizenship is the right of asylum.

We call basic rights the basic rules governing the legal position of individuals provided by the constitutional provisions of a state and including direct obligations for the behavior of the state. These basic rights can apply to all the people staying in a country or just to its citizens. Therefore they can encompass human rights as well as civil rights.

The inclusion of human rights in international law has linked the nations' codified basic rights to the international law's codified human rights. Thus we label human rights in a narrow sense those rights that either are part of customary international law or have been specifically set down in global or regional international law treaties.

ACCESSIBILITY TO REASONS AND THE POWER TO BIND

The core of human rights—acknowledging humans as free and equal persons whose integrity is to be protected by the government and who have a right to a share in making political decisions—is the main standard measuring the legitimacy of political rule today. This insight is becoming more and more prevalent, even though the thought of universal validity of human rights repeatedly stumbles on resistance. This resistance is derived primarily from the fact that the grounds for human rights are contained in European—more precisely the Judaic-Christian—tradition's idea of human dignity. This idea, so it is interjected, must not be covered over with that of other cultures. Yet this resistance should not lead to a denial of universal human rights, but should instead be made so applicable that a formulation accessible to reasons for human rights is sought.

No specific globally compelling reason for human rights can be furnished with binding authority, either in the domestic order or in international law. Pointing to human dignity does not change the fact that the basic rights of a modern constitutional nation as well as the human rights of modern international law must be expressed in a way accessible to reasons. This is required by the religious neutrality of the constitutional nation as well as the neutrality of international law toward the variety of human traditions, religions, and cultures.

But accessibility to reasons should not be taken for indecisiveness. Instead, it is very necessary for the sake of clarity of the concept of human rights to determine the content of the concept of human dignity that preceded it.

Every tradition has a contributory share in this. The tradition going back to Kant presents the thought that humans, as autonomous beings possessing reason's self-given law, are ends in themselves and must therefore never be considered mere means. The modern era's tradition of human rights endows this refusal to make humans instruments with a legal structure, and is often linked to an understanding of human rights as mere defensive rights. The core of human rights is seen as protection of individual liberty against interference by government force.

A Christian, trained in the Reformation tradition, will transcend this view and see that human dignity means that humans are understood to be beings who are not merged with any others but rather point beyond all given conditions, definitions, or achievements. This transcending character links the dignity of human beings to the dignity of all creatures, for all of creation points to the creator to whom creation owes its being. Yet humans are the beings who can behave reflexively to their self-transcendence, act in accordance with it, or fail to achieve it altogether.

One aspect of human dignity is that humans can fail to achieve their own dignity. Nevertheless, no earthly entity has the right to deny humans their dignity. Instead, the Reformation differentiation between the person and the person's works gains practical weight precisely in view of human dignity. Nor can any worldly entity derive the right from a person's unworthy behavior to declare that person without value.

Such an understanding of human value will also be the basis for all defense against interference in the realm of personal liberty, although it will not define this liberty as exclusively individual. Human dignity takes shape in coexistence. Human rights in the service of human dignity can also be measured by how far they support coexistence. In this respect human rights are not only defensive rights of the individual against the state but also, simultaneously, tasks in shaping political behavior.

ETHICS, RESPONSIBILITY, POWER

The insights gained in the study of human rights must be increased in the face of new challenges, the result of two threatening developments: (1) the violence with which human civilization endangers the natural foundations of life, and (2) the violence humans employ against each other. Violence against humanity and nature make the search for a basic core of ethical orientation inevitable.

I call this basic core "planetary ethos"; this term is meant to underline that the living space of planet earth as a whole has been entrusted to our care. Working to achieve a planetary ethos is today the most important task of ethics. Against the background of the descriptions of human dignity and human rights I will explain the new task of ethics.

I label "ethics" as the thinking about human responsibility. This responsibility reaches as far as the means of exercising human power does. As long as human power confines itself to the aftereffects of coexistence with the nearest neighbor, as long as its consequences are applied to those who are in this world with us, to that extent human responsibility is also limited. When the possibility for the human exercise of power widens, however, to the extent that it affects the whole globe, the lives of future generations of humans (and indeed, not just human lives but nonhuman lives as well), then the range of responsibility in space and time grows as well.

I understand "power" to be the human ability to realize self-imposed goals and to develop, prepare, and use the means to achieve these goals. Power is therefore more than the ability to carry out specific purposes against opposition.

Power is the circumstance that we can in fact control our methods of behavior. A mother has power—to use a simple example—not just when she forces a child to eat what's on the plate despite his or her protests, with the ominous threat that there would be no desert until the plate is clean. A mother's power in this case consists of the fact that she can even put some food on the table. In personal as well as political life, there are many situations when even this power is lacking.

Thus, power can be grasped as the ability to influence and shape our environment, the reality surrounding us. This ability has achieved an intensity in our present circumstances that no longer stops at the boundaries of human life. And it has achieved a range that no longer stops at the border of nations, continents, or religions. One example of increased ability to shape our environment is the plan to allow a dead pregnant woman to carry her baby to term. The increased range of human power is shown by space travel and, drastically, by the ozone hole.

These examples also make more obvious how the expansion of power also increases its discordance. The expansion of power leads to increased violence. Our increased behavioral possibilities are accompanied by a growth in destructive potential. With increased freedom our ability to limit freedom and make humans the object of our will to rule also increases. Progress in the technical mastery of nature has been accompanied by strides in destroying nature. With the refinement of weapons has grown their deadly effects.

Three responses can be made to this discordance in power: (1) cynical continuation in using power with acceptance of its destructive effects; (2) general renunciation of power; and (3) altering the use of power with the goal of decreasing the consequences inimical to life.

Religions always have been associated with all three responses, even to this day. They support the cynical forms of power and intensify the willingness to use power against humanity and nature. Both Saddam Hussein and George Bush claiming God's help in the 1991 Gulf War, or the unholy mixture of religion and nationalism in the destroyed Yugoslavia present us with depressing proof.

But general renunciation of power is also alive in religions. It is encountered everywhere where people voluntarily cede their chances to act and succeed. Yet this way of acting—as exemplified in mendicant orders, communes, or peace churches—is always confined to minorities in a social environment in which power is used. It is embedded in a society in which children are conceived and born, food is planted and harvested, the means of justice established and carried through. The renunciation of power is therefore dependent on the use of power, just as, conversely, the use of power depends on the fact that it will be faced with the critical mirror of general renunciation of power. This is the only way the critical testing and altering of human use of power occurs. Without such testing the use of human power becomes destructive and inimical to life.

THE CONCEPT OF POWER

Since the beginning of political ethics, one of its key themes has been the relationship between power and violence. "Violence" is derived from the Indo-Germanic root "*val*," also the origin of the Latin verb *valere* (strong, powerful, healthy). The word was originally used in terms of personal freedom rather than for legal affairs. Using "violence" was only considered illegal when it involved additional factors that gave it a malicious character damaging the legal rights of someone else.

This use of the word was so strange to the Roman legal tradition that it was used to translate very different Latin terms. First it was used for *potestas,* thus defining particular political positions of ruling, but in the course of the Middle Ages that definition was supplanted with the word *power.* This liberated "violence" to function as translation for *violentia,* defining direct bodily harm. Yet "violence" also continued to be used for the political exercise of power, as talk of the three constitutional national authorities—legislative, executive, and judiciary—and the related concept of the division of authority demonstrates.

The many meanings of "violence" accompanies the term to the present day. For this book, "violence" in the sense of *violentia* is the principal use. Yet many questions remain even if one uses this as a basis, most importantly, the problem of whether the concept "violence" is limited in all cases to direct and intentional physical injury. As much as violence against persons is in the foreground, there is little cause to exclude intentional damage to things. And even if physical injury is at the forefront of the concept of violence, the aspect of intentional mental injury can never be completely eliminated.

But above all it must be remembered that direct personal violence is not only employed individually but also collectively. True, basic moral intuitions and fully developed moral systems agree that they reject physical use of violence—especially in the form of killing violence. At the same time they find it necessary to arrive at different judgments regarding exceptions like individual self-defense and collective defense. The most powerfully effective historical form of collective use of violence is war. In the ethical tradition, the most expansive treatment has repeatedly been given to the question of whether and under what circumstances the use of violence in war can be justified. The answers range from a basic affirmation of this commanded use of violence, to specifying criteria according to which an individual is morally permitted to participate, to the rejection in principle of all violence, including that commanded by the state (see chapter 4).

This ethical controversy is caused by the ubiquity of violence. No human beings can decide whether they even want to begin with violence, for there is no situation totally devoid of violence. Among the concrete issues that confront humans during their lifetime is not only whether they wish to withdraw from continued violence by choosing nonviolence for themselves. They must also decide how they can oppose existing violence and decrease it. The dilemma always becomes pointed when one must ask whether the use of violence as a means to end violence is appropriate or even inevitable. The issue is posed primarily on the three levels of (1) personal self-defense, (2) the prosecution of the government monopoly on violence, and (3) the counterviolence of resistance and revolution.

Another question needing solution is whether structured violence should come to the aid of direct personal violence. The proposal to talk of structural violence is derived from the observation that humans are often impaired in their choices of lifestyles not so much by direct pressure from other individuals as by structural pressures, which force the concrete form of their lives to lag behind the choices that should really be open to them in their time.

Johan Galtung used this observation to propose an abstract definition:

> Violence exists when humans are so influenced that their actual somatic and spiritual self-actualization is less than their potential self-actualization.[2]

This proposed definition is certainly so far out that the concept loses any distinguishing marks. It becomes especially impossible to distinguish nonviolent from violent acts on the basis of that definition. But since this distinction is indispensable, it is advisable to limit the use of "violence" in the sense of *violentia* to direct bodily injury of every kind to persons, and to intentional damage to things. The questions that Galtung allocated to the concept of structural violence are in fact to be seen as problems of justice. Galtung's proposed expansion of the concept of violence causes more harm than good.

In the perception of acts of violence, personal violence against persons and against things takes precedence as a rule. Yet the fact that the expansion of industrial civilization has produced increasingly destructive consequences makes it imperative to pay more attention than ever to violence against nature. It is not always as obvious as in the clearing of rain forests. It frequently bears a intermediary character—as in the case of energy use, the side effects of which are the production of carbon dioxide and its related climate changes. In the technical world the indirect violence against nature surpasses by far the damage of direct violence. The amount of energy claimed for use by society constitutes one of the most important indicators of violence against nature emanating from that society.

MINIMIZING VIOLENCE

The ubiquity of violence was countered by Jesus in the Sermon on the Mount with the image of nonviolence. In the voluntary renunciation of violent defense and in love of enemy is the beginning of a new world arising out of the old. In the midst of irrationality the rationality of God's kingdom is exhibited.

This counterimage cannot be maintained without consequences to the political behavior of Christians. True, one cannot proclaim the renunciation of violence for everyone in a world still shaped by violence. The explanation for such a universal renunciation of violence would in truth have the effect of demanding the victims of violence to come to terms with what is being done to them. Such a demand to suffer would be irresponsible, for the willingness to suffer cannot be commanded, nor is it always in every way the right response to injustice. The Sermon on the Mount is not a simple proclamation of universal renunciation of violence but rather calls for persistent and imaginative efforts to decrease violence. Decreasing violence is an obligatory goal of historical dealings.

That public policy must serve the reduction and prevention of violence between people is an old insight. That is why one of the achievements of the modern state is that it dammed up violence—primarily in the form of feuds among its members—by means of government monopoly on violence. Yet this example points at the same time to the ambivalence of violence. The two forms of government monopoly on violence—police and military—use the threat or actual use of violence to prevent an outbreak of violence or to punish acts of violence.

But the danger is that police methods to abate violence by force actually result in increasing it. It is not just dictatorships that are familiar with this reversal. The military application of the state's monopoly on violence is known to lead to the intensification of violence rather than to the prevention and end of violence.

Thus the violence dilemma becomes acute. On the one hand, in the most extreme cases violence can only be ended by violence. On the other hand, violence and counterviolence are caught in a devil's spiral of increased involvement. Many ethical positions on violence solve the dilemma by making one of the two into absolutes.

Yet one cannot evade the dilemma. One can only try to lessen it by taming violence. Taming violence occurs primarily by educating people to behave nonviolently and by making the law supreme. Among the means of control are police precautionary measures against acts of violence and military securing of peace. These violent government measures must be tied firmly to the duty to prevent violence and to decrease it.

A decisive criterion to evaluate education and political behavior is whether they encourage nonviolent behavior and contribute to the decrease in violence. Although in the past these tasks were carried out with regard to violence between people only, in this time of massive threats to our environment decreasing violence against nature has become an important goal.

One of the most important missions of our time is to minimize violence in this comprehensive sense.

POWER AND VIOLENCE

What is the relation of power to violence? Recent political theory has developed two types of response. The one views violence as an indispensable instrument of political power, the other distinguishes power from violence by pointing to power's nonviolent resources. The former is represented by Max Weber, the latter by Hannah Arendt.

Max Weber starts with a limited concept of power. Power to him is not the general disposing of possible actions, but instead "the chance within a social relationship to carry out one's own will even against resistance, no matter what this chance is based on."[3]

With regard to political organizations, the decisive condition for success in carrying on the organization's will is contained in the threat and use of force. In the transition to the modern territorial state, the violence of many political organizations inside the territory—feudal rights—is eliminated by a legitimized monopoly on violence. Thus the modern state is the political organization that in its territory has control of the "monopoly of legitimate physical force."[4] The interpretation of the government's monopoly on violence as "monopoly of legitimate physical violence"[5] moves political power and collective use of force very close together.

State monopoly is not explained on the grounds of the state's duty to delegitimize and dam up violent activity in its own territory. Rather, it is explained on the basis that political organizations distinguish themselves from other organizations by controlling these particular power resources. The consequences are necessarily that the use of violence in the name of political organizations must be evaluated differently in ethical terms from other forms of violence. The danger in this kind of thinking is that it can lead to blunting the perception of government-ordered violence. In extreme cases it can even lead to legitimizing crimes committed in obedience to the state.

It is true that the close connection between power and violence is also presented with exactly contradictory intention. When principled pacifists present the thesis that all government power is based on violence, then to them the consequence—based on the principle of nonviolence—is their attempt to withdraw from all participation in the use of government power, even though they never quite succeed in doing so, as they themselves concede.

Hannah Arendt refutes the close and exclusive connection of power and violence. Violence is to be interpreted in terms of its character as instrument. It is dependent on instruments and is employed in the framework of an end-means relationship.

Power, on the other hand, is determined by its institutional character. It relies on the fact that a majority of people accept its use. That concept of power is the result of an analysis of political connections. A broader access to the phenomenon of power than was proposed in this chapter demonstrates that power certainly includes a particular relationship of ends and means. I had therefore defined power as the ability to act that permits humans to actualize self-chosen goals. Hannah Arendt's observation that power does not depend on particular instruments immediately available to a single individual—for instance, money or military violence—is pertinent even within my definition.

Political power bears an institutional character, is secured through institutions, and is dependent on the agreement to that institution on the part of those subjected to that power. The size of political power is consequently measured by the number of supportive followers, but the size of violence is measured by the strength of the instruments employed.

In accordance with this differentiation, the necessary precondition for all social arrangement is power and certainly not violence. Political power is based on a legitimacy resulting from the past, namely the historically developed support of a majority of people. There can be no such past-related legitimacy for violence. Moreover, the use of violent means can be justified only with a view to future results. Hannah Arendt does not exclude the possibility of justifiable use of violence in principle. But she does reject a theory that defines the state as a political organization by virtue of, and therefore dependent on, physical violence.

This view leads to a great skepticism regarding the expectation that less violent political circumstances can ensue from a violent revolution. Rather, revolutionary violence, if it is successful, leads precisely to the result that "the world has become more violent than it was."[6]

Hannah Arendt's objection to Max Weber's way of thinking appears convincing to me. She does not deny that in certain situations the threat and use of violence can be appropriate and even inevitable. But she ties this acknowledgment of violence to a strict duty to justify it. And she dissolves the tight connection of power and violence by pointing out that political power, like the other forms of power, is based on different sources than that of violence.

Our most recent history offers impressive evidence for the differentiation of political power and violence. When the one-party dictatorships in Central and East Europe could no longer depend on the support of a sufficient number of people, the means of violence at their disposal were no longer any use either. Their power had eroded so far that the system of rule by violence could no longer be maintained.

PLANETARY ETHOS

More careful distinction must be made between power and violence than frequently occurs. This applies especially at a time when the power of humans has been deeply changed by the possibilities of behavior opened to them by technology. Human power is no longer restricted to a narrow sphere but instead applies to the earth as a whole. And the range of human responsibility has grown commensurately.

Due to increased human possibility for action, the planet earth and its biosphere have become a living room that demands our responsibility. This responsibility applies not just to human life or only to certain aspects of life but to all of life. I have summarized human responsibility grown out of the additional human power as "planetary ethos." I call an ethic of responsibility that really confronts the intensity and extent of the human use of power at the present time "planetary ethic."

A planetary ethic turns to the question of how life can be preserved and enabled in this living room of the earth. This subject can no longer be resolved in exclusively regional, cultural, or religious circles. Instead, it requires dialogue and an understanding across regional, cultural, and religious lines. They need not in any way lead to uniformity in all ethical issues.

There is no need for unity about the rules regulating the different political, cultural, and religious communities' notions of good and successful life. Instead, agreement must be reached only about the principles required for the coexistence of different people in the one and only living room. These principles are derived from humanity's responsibility for the rights of future generations and for the maintenance of the foundation for natural life. Agreement must be sought on specific basic issues of justice. Diversity remains possible in the various ideas of a successful and good life.

"PROJECT WORLD ETHOS"

The discussion on a planetary ethos owes much to the Catholic theologian Hans Küng's proposed "project world ethos." Approval of his intention, however, does not exclude critique. My criticism is that Küng does not take the ethical plurality in today's world seriously enough.

In the modern world, not only different religious traditions but also different "secular humanisms" confront each other. We even have to deal with different ethical orientations within one and the same religion, as can be observed clearly in Christianity. And even a relatively closed community of faith like the Ro-

man Catholic Church is marked by notable polyphony, especially in the field of ethics. All of this can be illustrated with
examples from political ethics as well as from sexual ethics.

I do not think that Küng's ethical unity is either possible or
necessary when measured against this religious and secular
multiformity. Nor do I think the unity he dreams of is desirable.
He states, for example, "that the one world in which we live
has a chance to survive when different, contradictory, or even
conflicting ethics no longer exist in it." [7]

I differ with him, for I do not believe that humanity's salvation should be sought in a conflict-free ethic, although, to be
sure, the different ethics should fight without using violence.
The tension between the different ethics will determine humanity's future. And there is no reason to regret it, since ethical
lessons can be learned only from this kind of disagreement.
That is why my counterthesis asserts that "the demand
for agreement on a planetary ethos must concentrate on the
minimal conditions necessary for the survival of humanity, the
preservation of nature, and the right of future generations
to live."

A group of American and German theologians—Leonard
Swidler, John Hick, Johannes Lähnemann, Jürgen Moltmann,
and Theo Sundermeier among others—supported Hans Küng's
project with the proposal that a "Universal Declaration of World
Ethos" should be formulated comparable to the "Universal Declaration of Human Rights" in importance. Carl Friedrich von
Weizsäcker made this proposal his own.

In order to evaluate this proposal, I shall take another look
at the historical development of human rights.

HUMAN RIGHTS AND PLANETARY ETHOS

The 1948 "Universal Declaration of Human Rights" is a pro-
grammatic text, not a treaty in international law. Yet the United
Nations has worked for the passage of human rights in the form

of binding treaties in international law from the very beginning. The most important step toward realization of this plan was passage of the two Human Rights Treaties in 1966.

Those who want to endow human rights with worldwide legal ties must exercise restraint, in view of their ethical basis, which can also be observed in the development of the U.N. documents on human rights. The modern concept of human rights presupposes the distinction between legality and morality—which can be counted as a specific achievement of the European Enlightenment. Yet differentiation does not mean a lack of relationship.

Moreover, human rights stand for the connection of law and ethics, although they are connected in such a way that the two cannot be melded into one. The connection of legality and morality is expressed in a manner accessible to reasons.

Article I of the Declaration on Human Rights of 1948 states, "All human beings are born free and equal in dignity and rights. They are endowed with reason and conscience and should meet each other in the spirit of brotherhood." This statement combines three ethical traditions. The claim that all human beings are born free and equal in dignity and rights ties in with the Jewish and Christian idea of all humans created in God's image. The statement that all human beings are endowed with reason and conscience uses the Enlightenment belief in reason. Pointing to the brotherhood that should be universal is reminiscent of the French Revolution and the labor movement.

From today's viewpoint, the environment from which these traditions were chosen seems much too narrow. Consciousness of human rights must be put on a much broader foundation today. Accessibility to reasons regarding human rights must include the diversity of cultures and religions on the globe. Expressing human rights should not ignore this diversity but rather remain open to it. That is precisely why we demand the highest degree of religious restraint and restraint in expressing our worldview when formulating laws and formulating human rights as well. That is the only way law can preserve its accessi-

bility to reasons and therefore also respect the connection of
law and ethics.

The paralleling of the Universal Declaration of Human Rights
and a universal declaration of world ethos presented in support
of Küng's world ethos project ignores the difference between
law and ethos, legality and morality. Such a proposal—Küng,
after all, subscribed to it, even if he did not originate it—is
based on presuppositions that are closer to natural rights thinking than to that of the Enlightenment.

Natural rights thinking starts with the idea that law and mor-
als have the same source, namely natural reason's open recognition of the good. Accordingly, because of their reason human
beings are capable of insights into the good, independent of
time and context. This theory does not take into account a plurality of ethical principles. The Enlightenment tradition, on the
other hand, reflects the fact that within a society—and even
more so in a worldwide society—there are always several ethical orientations side by side.

The task of law is precisely that of enabling the coexistence
of different people. To be sure, this law functions only when the
consensus regarding basic preconditions to the law are constantly renewed in every community under the law. To that extent, ethics and law remain connected. Yet this consensus can
be renewed without imposing the law. Heeding the difference
between ethics and law is an important condition for freedom.
If this difference were ignored, an ethos—no matter how well
intentioned—could have consequences that violate the ethos.
If the ethos had at its disposal means of coercion comparable
to the means of coercion available to law, it would lose its ethical character.

ETHICAL DIMENSIONS OF HUMAN RIGHTS

I hold fast to the conclusion that a planetary ethos—a world
ethos, in the language of Hans Küng—is called for urgently. Its

task is not to smooth out the ethical differences between religions and cultures in the world, but rather to develop those principles necessary for the common life of human beings, the rights of future generations, and the preservation of nature, and to contribute to their binding force. These principles should be distinguished from the rules that are developed as answers to the search for a successful and good life in particular political, cultural, or religious communities.

One of these principles is respect for the equal dignity of all human beings and thus respect for basic human rights. Yet they are not identical in their function and content with the international catalogues of human rights. Instead, for the sake of freedom, the difference between legality and morality must be preserved. That is why it is neither appropriate nor helpful to put a "Universal Declaration of World Ethos" and the "Universal Declaration of Human Rights" on the same level.

Moreover, one should first ask, on the level of human rights, "Do the legal instruments of the international law community have to be expanded, half a century after the Universal Declaration of Human Rights?"

In my opinion this question should be answered in the affirmative. Expansion is particularly necessary in three areas:

- First, the international law community must expand its means to prevent or stem violent international and national conflicts.
- Second, the planetary duty to protect nature must be inculcated and carried out.
- Third, new instruments must be created to put a stop to the industrial nations' exploitation of economic superiority, and to contribute to a greater measure of justice in economic relations.

When I stress the difference between law and ethos, I certainly do not claim that they are unrelated, and that too is obvious in the development of human rights, for during the past fifty years human rights have attained a noteworthy measure of indirect ethical significance. The binding function of human rights thinking has gained importance precisely because in modern times various ethical convictions with equal claims to validity have appeared side by side. Although they themselves affirm rights the acknowledgment of which does not depend on fulfilling specific obligations, they do give rise to several moral—and that means they cannot be set into laws—individual obligations. Among these duties are the conduct of a lifestyle in responsible freedom, the mutual recognition of human beings as equals, defense of those whose basic rights are being violated, the overcoming of all forms of deprivation and discrimination, as well as taking part in politics.

In contradistinction to a positivist separation of law and morality, the particular significance of human rights is that it makes their connection obvious. It is not a coincidence that the decisive stimulus for including human rights in international law came out of the experience that a total separation of law and morality leads to a total destruction of law. That is why to this very day human rights are linked to not only the legal-ethical question of whether the various human, cultural, and religious traditions can find agreement on their legal content, but also the more far-reaching question of whether it is possible to have a common ethos despite the immense difference in basic ethical convictions on earth. The development of human rights awareness points in that direction.

The core of human rights already points to an overlapping area between the various basic convictions on ethics, in which the beginnings of a planetary ethos stand out. The basic elements of a planetary ethos can be detected in the recognition of inalienable human dignity as well as the freedom, equality, and participatory rights of all humans. Moreover, nothing provides more motivation to strive for such an ethos and—linked to it—for a global acknowledgment of human rights than the global prevalence of modern industrial civilization. Legal regulations and ethical convictions are necessary in equal measure to control this industrial civilization.

Changes in ethical attitudes also lead to reevaluation of human rights in important areas. It is necessary to point out, first of all, the consequences of an understanding of human rights these changes connote for the relations between men and women. True, explanations of human rights have from the beginning claimed all humans are born with equal rights. Yet for centuries the unequal treatment of women was continued in important civil areas. Women were denied the right to vote until the twentieth century; in domestic disagreements, family law gave the man the deciding vote; in labor law, unequal pay for equal labor continues to be tolerated.

For the territory of the Federal Republic of Germany, the provision for equal rights in the constitution[8] signified an important breakthrough. Yet it took decades before it was carried out in critical areas of the law as well as in concrete reality, and this has still not been fully successful. Many countries, including the United States, are still far removed from the realization of these standards of equality which—just as in our constitution—can be found in International Conventions on Human Rights. Going beyond just the general prohibition against discrimination, the 1948 Universal Declaration of Human Rights already specifically called for equal pay for equal labor.[9] The International Treaty on Economic, Social, and Cultural Rights of 1966 obligates the participating nations to secure the equality of men and women in the exercise of all rights established in the treaty.[10] Step by step, the insight has gained ground in the international legal community that only when the rights of women are not only proclaimed but are actually honored in equal manner to the rights of men can there be talk of human rights.

The inclusion of human rights in international law prepared the way for the creation of a planetary ethos. Changes in ethical principles have had an effect on the further development of human rights standards. Yet one should not underestimate the ambivalence that accompanies the double applicability of human rights in a legal and ethical sense. It leads to repeated attempts to include in the concept of human rights all the goals that should be given ethical priority. But the consequence would be the weakening, if not the eroding, of the legal character of human rights, and perhaps dissolving it altogether.

THIRD GENERATION OF HUMAN RIGHTS

The discussion of human rights of the "third generation" is particularly important. While the civil and political rights of freedom ("first generation") as well as the civil human rights ("second generation") considered the individual person to be the bearer of human rights, the "third generation" refers to nations and ethnic groups as bearers of human rights.

Among the rights of the "third generation," according to the proposals discussed in the United Nations, are the rights to development, to peace, and to environmental protection as well as the right to a share of "the common inheritance of humanity," meaning the resources of the ocean depths, the use of outer space, and also natural and cultural goods of the earth. These demands are very significant. They are the more convincing in that the various nations have highly unequal access to the earth's resources and the use of them.

Discrimination against the southern hemisphere is the major topic of the "third generation" of human rights. This discrimination has to be overcome if human rights are to apply to the whole globe and are to be protected effectively. That is why it is justifiable to link the large themes of peace, development, environmental protection, and use of resources to human rights.

Nevertheless, to simply parallel the "third generation" of human rights with the other two generations cuts both ways. Human rights would then be interpreted in the sense of collective rights. But as collective rights they do not bear a character predating the state, and they are not withdrawn from the control of nations. They would then be much more the subject of political disputes and political decisions. Undoubtedly the character of individual and civil rights predating nations was at first the result of sharp political debates. Yet there were unequivocal reasons for its success. Basic rights acknowledged as preceding the national state are tied to the individual person as legal subject, and see to it that the dignity of all human beings is respected and that their freedom, their equality, and their share in the common life is supported. Personal rights of freedom and civil rights—in contrast to the solidarity rights of the "third generation"—are applied to the individual person.

With regard to the "third generation", one should rather refer to "standards of human rights."[11] For the sake of human rights, the matter of these political demands is one of great urgency.

THE RIGHTS OF NATURE

An expansion of human rights into yet another direction was proposed out of a similar ethical interest to supplement human rights with both the rights of future generations and the rights of nature. In this case too the intention makes sense: the presently living generation's obligation must be made more obvious. When making decisions, the present generation must take into consideration the claim of future generations to at least those rights of freedom now being applied to themselves. And their duty not just to use nature as a means to satisfy human interests, but also to guard nature's own interests and preserve them should be underlined. Yet dressing such duties as laws—instead of provisional national objectives on the one hand, commandments and prohibitions on the other—leads to a metaphorical use of the concept of law, which weakens the meaning of law.

Although human rights are suitable for strengthening the awareness of a planetary ethos, they themselves are threatened when they are simply made into instruments of such an ethos.

The tendency to declare everything ethically desirable "human rights" or parallel with human rights hollows out the legal character of human rights.

For that reason I plead for limiting the concept of human rights to basic individual and social rights borne by individual persons. And I further plead for not including into the concept of human rights all thoughts that have an appropriate place in planetary ethos.

RELATIVE UNIVERSALISM

I cling to another conclusion: the demands of a planetary ethos can neither be placed on the same level as human rights, nor can they be found in all human rights catalogues or even be included in them. Moreover, it is time to formulate independent, more far-reaching principles about which the different cultures and religions can agree should be sought. Our discussion on human rights has provided important incentives to do so, for it has made more obvious that these principles must include the mutual acknowledgment of equal dignity of all humans and the mutual encouragement of their freedom, equality, and active participation in their common life. Furthermore, these principles must place particular stress on the equal dignity of women, the support of social justice, and the protection of nature.

Can one expect that such principles will be acknowledged as universal? Once again a comparison with human rights gives rise to skepticism on this point. Although the universal character of human rights has not been in question for a long time, it has in the past few decades fallen into a hash of relativistic critique.

European universalism was for a long time of the opinion that European cultural tradition provided the access to moral insights that could be made universal and thus applied to all humans. According to universalists, as long as other cultural traditions do not arrive at the same insights it is proof of their inferiority. The caste system in India or the surgical removal of the clitoris on Arab women are used as signs that Indian or Arab culture is at an inferior level.

This linkage between human rights consciousness and an imperialist universalism of culture has of course given rise to a countermovement that radically states that moral convictions gain their validity solely from their particular cultural living conditions. Thus there are no ethical norms independent of context. Every attempt to bring about an agreement regarding them is doomed to failure.

This radical relativism is, naturally, as wrong as radical universalism. Along with Küng, I oppose them with the fact that there is an overlapping area in which the moral convictions of diverse cultural and religious traditions meet. Relativism, moreover, withdraws from the task of contributing to the coexistence of different people, and thus denies itself the task of giving the pluralism of today's world society a life-enhancing shape and worthwhile living conditions.

Relativists frequently work with an abstract concept of "context," for they give the appearance that the life contexts—limited by space and time—in which humans move and act are hermetically sealed from the outside world and marked by cultural homogeneity inside. That is in no way the case. Instead, every context is always meshed in many ways with other contexts.

Moreover, today one must reckon with multiculturalism within even living communities, which makes the search for mutually shared convictions even more difficult. It is well known that there are growing numbers of multicultural or multireligious families who need such an area. The relations between generations are also marked to a growing extent by cultural conflicts.

A radical relativism is possible only in closed cultures. The ancient Greeks could label all foreigners barbarians. Only gradually did philosophy raise the questions of whether common membership in the human species is stronger than the differences between Greeks and barbarians. The Hopi name for themselves and other groups of native Americans is simply "the people." That other peoples existed had absolutely no relevance to their cultural self-understanding.

When the Spanish and Portuguese conquered Latin America, the question was soon asked whether natives could even be considered human—and so be converted to Christianity. One arrived—in theory—at the conclusion that they too should be considered human, which did not, however, improve their circumstances much.

These kinds of historical precedents produced the insight that despite all the cultural and religious variations, a very few culture-transcending principles must be acknowledged as essentially applying to the life and integrity of all human beings. The Universal Declaration of Human Rights draws consequences for law from these principles, the result of a historical learning process that led to "relative universality." [12]

I use the term "relative universality" for two reasons. In contrast to a radical relativism it points to necessary and possible ethical insights, transcending culture and religion, which are so basic that they can also attain a legally binding form.

In contrast to a radical universalism, it points to the fact that such ethical insights and legal norms are also historically impermanent, thus relative. Consensus on such insights and norms grows out of the diversity and the richness of cultural traditions and religious convictions, and must be anchored and repeatedly embedded in this diversity. Those who want to strengthen the universal application of ethical insights and standards of human rights must deal with the particularity of these traditions and convictions. Those who desire to reduce religious or cultural traditions to what can be expressed in common would plug up the only sources from which a planetary ethos could flow.

Only by going through the particularities of culture and religions, not bypassing them, can a consensus on standards of human rights and other elements of a planetary ethos be developed. A relative universalist does not assume that a direct insight into the ethos connecting all humans exists independent of context. He or she does not share the rational optimism of the natural rights tradition. Nor does he know of any agency that could guarantee a consensus independent of context. The United Nations cannot take over a secularized papal teaching office. Such a consensus, therefore, can only be—at all times capable of being superseded and surpassed—the result of understandings that have included the participation of the various cultural and religious traditions.

A planetary ethos will not prevail by way of abstract doctrine. It will only take shape when it is given life in communities in which people form their moral convictions and transmit them. Only when the human beings in oral tradition communities develop their identity and achieve it, and become open to the common tasks of humankind will the obligations to humanity and nonhuman nature enter into moral consciousness. That is why it is important to anchor the further development of ethical orientations not only in religious communities, but also in secular-humanist groups.

The conciliatory process for justice, freedom, and the preservation of creation that the World Council of Churches touched on in 1983 has special significance in that it acknowledged these communities and groups as independent subjects of judgmental formation. Special attention was paid to the circumstances of people who are forced to suffer the most from injustice and the destructive consequences of today's world civilization—the victims of hunger and exploitation, torture and dictatorships, pollution of the environment, and war.

Today's task is to transcend the borders of Christian churches and reach an understanding with other religions and with secular humanism regarding the principles of a planetary ethos. Yet even in this step, concern should be maintained for the groups and communities in which the moral convictions of humans are born. And once again we should listen with particular attention to those whose suffering from turmoil and injustice obligates us to provide a new beginning.

The planetary ethos should not be drafted by an elite functioning as proxy. It should be anchored in a broad drafting process in which the diversity of living convictions and fellowships of suffering is heard. Not an explanation of a world ethos by a small commission of people but a widespread discussion about the responsibility facing humanity is what we hope for and must strive for.

All attempts to formulate the elements of a planetary ethos are also colored by the cultural world from which they stem. This can be illustrated by Hans Küng's proposal to combine the imperatives common to all world religions. According to Küng, they are "(1) Do not kill; (2) do not lie; (3) do not steal; (4) do not commit adultery; (5) honor your parents and love your children." [13] This list is recognizable as being rooted in Israel's Ten Commandments and in Christian history. Küng expresses them as ethical rules, but fails to answer precisely those controversial ethical questions to be found at this level. I will refer to his list for examples of open questions:

- Are there exceptions to the prohibition on killing?
- Is all sexuality outside the heterosexual monogamous marriage adultery?
- Where do the parents' demands for obedience end, or the demands on children to care for them?

Küng's "Project World Ethos" suggests a lack of ambiguity that does exist, and he lays claim to a universality that does not exist.

What is to be remembered is that there is an overlapping area in which ethical convictions of various cultures and religions meet. This overlapping can be formulated more easily at the level of principles required for the coexistence of different people, rather than at the level of rules intended to ensure a uniform behavior in practical matters.

In view of the challenges of the present time, this overlapping area must be widened and strengthened. Yet the attempts to fix its contents will always have a prospective character. That is not a bad thing. Only where variety is alive can an insight into the basic conditions of coexistence of different people grow. Only where people display their difference can they learn that there are minimum standards for coexistence, and that coexistence is endangered or destroyed if these are not obeyed.

Out of the perspective developed in this book, I will list ten principles for coexistence as initial steps in a planetary ethos:

- Honor the dignity of all human beings as well as the dignity of nature.
- Respect the freedom, equality, and participatory rights of all human beings.
- Exercise tolerance toward the convictions and lifestyles of others.
- Take the life and the right to life of the next generation as seriously as your own.
- Defend the rights and the future of weaker human beings.
- Take part in dismantling neglect and discrimination.
- Carry on personal, social, and political conflicts without violence.
- Make use of nature in a manner commensurate with its dignity and contribute to the natural foundation of life.
- Take part in social and political responsibility.
- Bear responsibility for how you use your freedom.

The starting points of a planetary ethos are respect for the dignity of nature and honoring the dignity of human beings. Minimizing violence against human beings and nature is its most important goal. No one is excluded from taking part, for everyone can contribute to the care of nature and the defense of human dignity.

Notes

CHAPTER 1. Violence and Intimacy as Entertainment

1. Hans Helmut Kohl, "Catastrophe(n) Journalismus," *Der Journalist* 7 (1988): 8–13.
2. Immanuel Kant, *Zum ewigen Frieden. Ein philosophischer Entwurf, 1795, 1796* (Darmstadt: 1968), 46.
3. Otto B. Roegele, "Verantwortung des Journalisten," in P. Schiwy and W. J. Schütz, eds., *Medienrecht. Stichwörter für die Praxis* (Neuwied: 1977), 211.
4. Ada Brandes, in *Die Stuttgarter Zeitung*, reprinted in *Der Journalist* 8 (1988): 42–43.
5. Ibid.
6. Helmut Simon, "Der Preis für die Freiheit steigt, wenn die Nachfrage sinkt. Anmerkungen zur Rolle der vierten Gewalt" in M. Buchwald, ed., *In bester Verfassung? Anmerkungen zum 40. Geburtstag des Grundgesetzes* (Gerlingen: 1989), 158.
7. Manfred Köhnlein, *Public Forum* (29 January 1993), 18.
8. Klaus Merten, in *Frankfurter Rundschau* (28 January 1993), 23.
9. Max Weber, "Politik als Beruf," in his *Gesammelte politische Schriften* (Tübingen: 1980), 551–52.
10. Klaus Bresser, in *Süddeutsche Zeitung* (3 April 1989).
11. Max Frisch, *Tagebuch 1946–1949*, vol. II/2 of *Gesammelte Werke* (Frankfurt: 1976), 369–70.

CHAPTER 2. Taking Liberties with Human Dignity

1. Dietrich Kurz in *Menschen im Sport 2000. Dokumentation des Kongresses* (Schorndorf: 1988), 128.

2. Ommo Grupe, in *Menschen im Sport 2000,* 45–46.
3. Robert N. Bellah et al., *Habits of the Heart: Individualism and Commitment in American Life* (New York: HarperCollins, 1986).
4. Michael Welker, *God the Spirit* (Minneapolis: Fortress Press, 1994).
5. The source is commentator Heinz Fallak.

CHAPTER 3. The Society of the Majority and the Minorities

1. Carl Zuckmayer, *Des Teufels General in drei Akten* (Frankfurt: 1977), 65–66.
2. Heinrich von Treitschke, "Unsere Aussichten," written in 1879, in W. Boehlich, ed., *Der Berliner Antisemitismus* (Frankfurt: 1965), 9.
3. Norbert Elias and J. L. Scotson, *Etablierte und Aussenseiter* (Frankfurt: 1990).
4. Ibid., 175.
5. Quoted by Christa Gürtler, *Gegen den schönen Schein Texte zu Elfriede Jelinek* (Frankfurt: 1990), 8.
6. Beate Winkler, "Kulturpolitik für eine multikulturelle Gesellschaft," in St. Ulbrich, ed., *Multikultopia. Gedanken zur multikulturellen Gesellschaft* (Vilsiburg: 1991), 294.
7. John Rawls, *Die Idee des politischen Liberalismus* (Frankfurt: 1992), 84–85.
8. Beate Winkler, "Kulturpolitik," 294.
9. Herman Lübbe, "Für eine europäische Kulturpolitik," in *Europäische Kultur. Das Zukunftsgut des Kontinents* (Gütersloh: 1990), 53.
10. Ibid., 55.
11. *Information fur die Truppe* 4 (1991): 6.

CHAPTER 4. A Look Back at the Gulf War

1. Hans Magnus Enzenberger in *Der Spiegel.*
2. Horst Eberhard Richter in *Publik Forum.*
3. *Friedensgutachten 1991* (Münster: 1991), 95.
4. *Die Unordnung der Welt und Gottes Heilsplan,* vol. 4 (Genf: 1948), 260.
5. Dietrich Vorwerk, in *Die Christliche Welt* 28 (1914), column 1069.
6. *Ökumenische Versammlung für Gerechtigkeit, Frieden, und Bewahrung der Schöpfung. Dresden-Magdeburg-Dresden. Eine Dokumentation* (Berlin: 1990), 17.

CHAPTER 5. Military Violence after the Cold War

1. Carl von Clausewitz, *Vom Kriege* (1832–1834; Frankfurt: 1981) vol. 8:674.

2. United Nations Charter.

3. Documented in the *Frankfurter Rundschau* (May 10, 1991).

4. United Nations Charter, Chapter VII, Art. 42ff.

5. Ibid., Chapter VII, Art. 43.

6. Ibid., Art. 47.

7. Ibid., Art. 51.

CHAPTER 7. Violence against Humanity and Nature

1. Immanuel Kant, "Grundlegung zur Metaphysik der Sitten," in vol. 7 of *Die Metaphysik der Sitten,* 10 volumes (1797, 1798; Darmstadt: 1968), 77.

2. Johan Galtung, "Gewalt, Frieden und Friedensforschung" in D. Senghaas, ed., *Kritische Friedensforschung* (Frankfurt: ?), 57.

3. Max Weber, *Wirtschaft und Gesellschaft. Grundriss der verstehenden Sociologie* (Tübingen: 1976), 28.

4. Ibid., 29.

5. Max Weber, "Politik als Beruf" in his *Gesammelte politische Schriften* (Tübingen: 1980), 506.

6. Hannah Arendt, *Mach und Gallate* (München: 1970), 80.

7. Hans Küng, *Project Weltethos* (München: 1990), 14.

8. Bonn Constitution, Article 3:2GG.

9. Ibid., Article 23:II.

10. Ibid., Article 3.

11. Eibe Riedel, *Theorie des politischen Liberalismus* (Berlin: 1986).

12. Jack Donnelly, *Universal Human Rights in Theory and Practice* (Ithaca, N.Y.: Cornell University Press, 1988).

13. Hans Küng, *Project Weltethos,* 82.

Index

American society. *See* U.S. situation
Anti-Semitism, 3–4, 55, 68, 76, 83, 116
Arendt, Hannah, 132, 133–34
Augustine, 88

Bach, Ulrich, 45
Balkan War, 77, 100, 109–12
Bellah, Robert N., 37
Bible, 29, 67–68, 79, 115
Bonhoeffer, Dietrich, 79
Brandes, Ada, 21
Bresser, Klaus, 27
Bulger, James, 1
Bush, George, 84, 97, 99, 127

Celebrities, 37–39
Children, 1–2
Christian tradition, 9, 30, 41, 45, 53–54, 63–64, 65, 67–70, 78, 79, 84, 86, 89, 91–92, 115–20, 123, 130, 145
Coexistence, 56, 70–73, 114, 149
Cold War aftermath, 6, 7, 39, 55, 97–101
Columbus, Christopher, 117
Culture of violence, xv

Darwin, Charles, 86
De Beauvoir, Simone, 58
Della Mirandola, Pico, 117
Democracy, 63–64
Descartes, René, 43
Dignity, 5, 9–11, 28, 41–42, 60, 63, 114–21, 139
Disabilities, 3, 44–45, 46
Discrimination, 57, 70, 116

East European situation, 5
Economics. *See* Market principle
Elias, Norbert, 57–59
English situation, 1, 57–58
Enlightenment, 9, 64, 70, 119–21, 137
Entertainment, violence in, xv, 2, 13–18, 19–25, 29–30
Environment, 3, 47–49, 100, 121, 135, 142, 143–44
Erasmus, 117
Ethics. *See also* Christian tradition; Dignity; Human rights; Just-war theory
    Christian, 30, 41, 85–94, 114–21
    defined, 125
    dignity vs. interests, 41–43
    generations of, 121, 142

Ethics. (*continued*)
  media ethics, 14–15, 23–30
  orientations, 114
  pacifist, 91–94
  peace-ethic, 101–06
  planetary, 125–27, 134–38, 140, 141
  universalist, 27–28, 144–49
Ethnic violence, 3, 5

Francis Suarez, 118
Francis of Victoria, 118
Freedom, 113–14, 123–25, 127
Frisch, Max, 30
Fundamentalism, 71–72, 86–88, 94–95

Galtung, Johan, 129–30
German situation, 3–4, 48, 49–50, 51–52, 55, 73, 101
  Bonn Constitution, 10, 17–18, 42, 64
Geyer, Alan, 82
Government action, 11, 50, 131, 132–33
Green, Barbara, 82
Grupe, Ommo, 35
Gulf War, 71, 75–79, 80, 82, 90, 94, 99, 109

Habermas, Jürgen, 18
Hobbes, Thomas, 188
Human rights, 9–10, 16–17, 60, 114, 121–25, 142–43
  international law and, 121–22, 139–42
  types of, 122–23, 138
  United Nations and, 136–38

Immigrants, 3, 49–50, 51–53
Individualism, 37, 49–50
Intimacy, 14
Israel, 76, 82, 83

Jelinek, Elfriede, 59
Jesus model, xi, 44–46, 130
Jewish tradition, 29, 41, 53, 67, 114, 115
Johnson, Ben, 31
Journalism, 13–18, 24–30
Just-war theory, 78–83, 85–94

Kant, Immanuel, 16, 93, 120–21, 124
Küng, Hans, 135–36, 138, 145, 148
Kurz, Dietrich, 33

Lifestyle, 6, 7–8, 36–39, 54, 113, 114, 140
Lübbe, Hermann, 66

MacIntyre, Alasdair, 70
Market principle, 8, 14–15, 21–22, 28–29, 39–40, 44
Media. *See* Entertainment
Military violence, 6, 102, 106–12, 131. *See also* War
Minorities, 51–60, 61, 70
More, Thomas, 117
Movies. *See* Entertainment
Multiculturalism, 60–73, 114, 145

Namibia, 106–07
Nature. *See* Environment
News reporting. *See* Journalism

Olympic model, xi, 40, 44–46, 47

Pacifism, 77, 82, 91–94
Pluralism, 26, 28
Postman, Neil, 18–19
Power, 100, 125–28, 132–34

Radke, Frank-Olaf, 61
Rawls, John, 64
Reformation, 86, 89, 119–20, 124–25

Relativism, 72, 144–46
Responsibility, ethics of, 34–36
Rights. *See* Human rights
Roegele, Otto B., 18

Saddam Hussein, 71, 75, 76, 84, 94, 127
Sexual violence, 2, 14–15, 20
Simpson, O. J., 13
Singer, Peter, 43
Sports, 31–41
Strangers, 68–70. *See also* Immigrants; Minorities

Television, 1, 2, 19, 20–21, 29–30 *See also* Entertainment

United Nations, 93
  Charter, 103–06
  Declarations, 10, 136–38, 146
  Gulf War role, 75, 76, 81, 100
  peacekeeping role, 6, 101–12
U.S. situation, 8, 55, 94, 97, 100, 141

Von Clausewitz, Carl, 99
Values, core, 63
Violence
  defined, 128–30
  depiction of, 16–17, 24–25, 77
  forms of, 2–6, 24
  power and, 126–28, 132–34
  nonviolent response, 91–93, 127, 131

War, 71–84, 89–90, 99, 104. *See also* Military violence; Just-war theory
Weber, Max, 26, 132
Weiss, Konrad, 82
Welker, Michael, 39
Winkler, Beate, 62, 64, 72
Women
  discrimination against, 58–59, 65
  violence against, 2

Youth violence, 1, 4, 23